UNRULY WOMEN: PERFORMANCE, PENITENCE, AND PUNISHMENT IN EARLY MODERN SPAIN

Unruly Women

Performance, Penitence, and Punishment in Early Modern Spain

MARGARET E. BOYLE

UNIVERSITY OF TORONTO PRESS
Toronto   Buffalo   London

ISBN 978-1-4426-4615-5

Printed on acid-free, 100% post-consumer recycled paper with
vegetable-based inks.

Library and Archives Canada Cataloguing in Publication

Boyle, Margaret E., 1983–, author
Unruly women : performance, penitence, and punishment in early
modern Spain / Margaret E. Boyle.

(Toronto Iberic)
Includes bibliographical references and index.
ISBN 978-1-4426-4615-5 (bound)

1. Spanish drama – Classical period, 1500–1700 – History
and criticism.   2. Women in literature.   3. Women – Institutional
care – Spain – History.   4. Women – Rehabilitation – Spain – History.
5. Women – Spain – Social conditions – 16th century.   6. Women –
Spain – Social conditions – 17th century.   I. Title.
II. Series: Toronto Iberic

PQ6102.B69 2014   862'.3099286   C2013-905688-2

University of Toronto Press acknowledges the financial assistance to its
publishing program of the Canada Council for the Arts and the
Ontario Arts Council.

Canada Council   Conseil des Arts
for the Arts   du Canada

University of Toronto Press acknowledges the financial support of the
Government of Canada through the Canada Book Fund for its
publishing activities.

Contents

Acknowledgments vii

Introduction 3

Part One

1 Gendering *Recogimiento* in Early Modern Madrid 19

    I Reforming Prostitutes: Madrid's Magdalen House 25

    II Reforming the Magdalen House: Madre Magdalena de
San Jerónimo's *galera* 30

    III *Recogimiento* as a Women's Practice 39

Part Two

2 Stage Widow in Pedro Calderón de la Barca's *La dama duende* 45

3 Dramatizing Women's Community in María de
Zayas's *La traición en la amistad* 62

4 Women's Exemplary Violence in Luis Vélez de Guevara's
La serrana de la Vera 77

Conclusion 96

Epilogue: "Bad Girls" of the Spanish *Comedia* 101

Contents

Appendix 1A. *Reason and Form of the Galera and
Royal House* (1608) 107

Appendix 1B. *Razón y forma de la galera y casa real* (1608) 113

Appendix 2A. *Historical Compendium and Instructive Manifesto on the
Origin and Foundation of the Royal House of St Mary Magdalene of the
Penitence, commonly known as the Recogidas of Madrid* 119

Appendix 2B. *Compendio histórico, y manifiesto instructivo del origen,
y fundación de la Real Casa de Santa María Magdalena de la Penitencia,
vulgo las Recogidas de Madrid* 123

Notes 127

Works Cited 145

Index 159

Acknowledgments

Research for this project was made possible with the support of the Program for Cultural Cooperation between Spain's Ministry of Culture and United States Universities and multiple grants from Emory University and Bowdoin College. I was also able to participate in the XXXI Jornadas de Teatro Clásico de Almagro sponsored by the Universidad de Castilla-La Mancha during an archival research trip in 2008. As the annual meeting was dedicated to my beloved *Damas en el tablado*, I am especially grateful for the opportunity to have experienced firsthand the masterful prowess of the *comedias'* heroines.

I have been fortunate to be surrounded by a strong and supportive team of colleagues. I am grateful to María M. Carrión for first shepherding me through the archives and into the world of early modern Spanish theatre. I am indebted to Karen Stolley for her intellectual generosity and her enduring support, and to Sharon T. Strocchia for her thoughtful advice and rigorous example. I am also thankful for the support I have received from my colleagues across campus at Bowdoin College, with special thanks to the Department of Romance Languages. I am likewise grateful for the encouraging feedback and suggestions I have received at the following conferences, where I presented chapters of my book: the Association for Hispanic Classical Theater, Grupo de Estudios de la Mujer en España y las Americas, the Modern Language Association, and the National Women's Studies Association. The editors at the *Bulletin of the Comediantes* kindly gave permission to reprint a revised version of chapter 4.

I am deeply appreciative of many fellow scholars of the *siglo del otro*, especially Ariadna García-Bryce, Gloria Hernández, Sherry Velasco, Lisa Vollendorf, Amy Williamsen, and the two anonymous readers at the University of Toronto Press for their insightful and energizing feedback on this project at its various stages. Several archivists and librarians in the United States and Spain provided insight into my research and writing process. I am especially grateful for the conversations I had during my visits to Madrid's National Library, the National Historical Archive, and the Royal Convent of la Encarnación in Madrid. I am grateful to the editorial team at the University of Toronto Press, including Barb Porter, Suzanne Rancourt, and Miriam Skey for their thoughtful commitment to my book. Ivan Karp and Corinne Kratz provided me with the tools and confidence to write the grants I needed to fund early research. I express my special gratitude to Michelle Beckett, Elizabeth Drumm, Hazel Gold, Jonathan Goldberg, Durba Mitra, Ana Isabel Montero, and José Quiroga for reading selections of this manuscript, and to my undergraduate students past and present for their lively questions and contagious enthusiasm. Finally, I thank and celebrate my family, friends, and colleagues for their support throughout the process of researching and writing this book, with special thanks to my parents Don and Gina Boyle, and also to Brittany Anderson-Cain, Bich Ngoc Cao, Ana Cara, Rachel Crothers, Ana María Díaz Burgos, Matthew Edwards, Omar Granados, Lisa Knisely, Rhia Lagarejos, Lynn Maxwell, Sandra Navarro, Patrick O'Connor, Mao Shiokura, and Patty Tovar, among many others.

I dedicate this book with love to Andrew and Nora.

UNRULY WOMEN: PERFORMANCE, PENITENCE,
AND PUNISHMENT IN EARLY MODERN SPAIN

Introduction

The actress Barbara Coronel (1643–91) began her career at age eleven alongside her parents, Agustin and Maria Coronel, in the company of Tomas Diaz in Seville. For fifteen years, the actress celebrated her success onstage and off while she managed her own troupe of actors in Valencia. On stage, she frequently and to much acclaim played the part of the *mujer varonil* (masculine woman). Coronel's cross-dressing also extended into her personal life, where she is said to have openly dressed and behaved as a man (Shergold and Varey 422). When her husband Francisco Jalon was murdered, Coronel was accused of the crime and called before the Inquisitional Tribunal in Guadalajara. Shortly before her scheduled execution, her well-known uncle, actor Cosme Pérez (better known as Juan Rana), made appeals on behalf of his niece and the Inquisition absolved her from the charges. According to Casiano Pellicer's account of the trial, it was the actors' dramatic talents that precipitated the change in ruling (28).[1]

Barbara Coronel's story illustrates the interconnected relationships between performance, penitence, and punishment in early modern Spain. Although it is difficult to indicate the exact reasons for reversing the charges against Coronel, the way in which the case positions the discourse of actors against the discourse of Inquisition highlights the powerful role of performance for both parties. What emerges most clearly from the case is the fact that Coronel's masculine behaviour framed her as a more likely candidate for murder. In early modern Spain, rehabilitation and punishment were elaborate and often highly regimented acts. Whether or not it was the actors' "performance" that reversed the Inquisitors' charges, this case also demonstrates how acts of rehabilitation and punishment were mutable and contradictory.

Among early modern Spanish society, a growing preoccupation with unruly women like Coronel fuelled the creation of various custodial institutions designed to house and rehabilitate women.[2] These institutions gained popularity beginning in the early sixteenth century as part of Counter Reformation projects; they included numerous types of institutions that varied from widows' asylums and refuges for battered wives to magdalen houses for prostitutes, orphanages, hospitals, and jails.[3] Frequently modelled on monastic discipline, the common, overarching goal of these institutions was the creation of a single-sex environment designed to address the particular physical, spiritual, moral, or economic deficiencies perceived to be experienced by women. Although new legal codes, royal decrees, and a proliferation of conduct literature tried to produce a more consistent morality, practices of rehabilitation for women were markedly inconsistent. Instead, early modern Spanish policies and politics suggest a varied, sometimes flexible, and often contradictory moral arrangement. The early modern Spanish subject was constructed through a variety of competing discourses, which both enforced and critiqued expected social behaviour. These tensions and contradictions – between charity, healing, and education, and control, punishment, and exclusion – produced what George Mariscal calls the *Contradictory Subjects* of early modern Spain.[4] Practices of rehabilitation for women were often inconsistent, given these competing values and expectations.

Unruly Women analyses the interconnected relationships among public theatre, custodial institutions, and women in early modern Spain in order to explore the contradictory practices of rehabilitation enacted by women both on and off stage. The book argues that women's performances of penitence and punishment should be considered a significant factor of early modern Spanish life. It pairs historical narratives and archival records with canonical and non-canonical theatrical representations of women's deviance and rehabilitation. The book takes into account the preponderance of defiant heroines imagined by the early modern theatre and housed in contemporary custodial institutions, and argues that rehabilitation must be understood in the frame of gender.[5] Although men and women are punished for crime, the book follows Elisabet Almeda's assertion that women's situations are unique since they violate both penal laws and social norms that dictate what it means to be feminine (*Mujeres y castigo*). This book focuses on women who inhabit and transgress the proscriptive roles produced for them by custodial institutions and the *comedia* as it joins two seemingly disparate spaces in which women play a critical role.

In early modern Europe, the regulation of moral behaviour was widely understood as a public concern. Spanish moralists like Juan Luis Vives, and his contemporaries Fray Luis de León, Gaspar de Astete, and Pedro Malón de Chaide, proffered advice on proper conduct and self-regulation.[6] The Counter Reformation in Spain was mobilized and implemented in no small part by means of a new legal code, the Nueva Recopilación de las leyes de estos reynos (New Compilation of the Laws of the Kingdoms), supplemented by the publication of numerous *edictos* and *pragmáticas* (royal decrees) designed to cleanse and order urban spaces. These new laws and decrees mainly targeted ethnic and religious minorities, the poor, and women.[7] By instilling clear moral values and ridding city streets of profane topics such as sex, illness, and crime, state and local officials aimed to project a new and confident sense of cleanliness and social order, a task frequently complemented by the activity of local custodial institutions.

What gives these institutions added significance is the complex, interdependent relationship they shared with public theatres.[8] Although moralists chastised popular playwrights for their public display of sinful behaviours on stage, revenue generated from these same popular *comedias* was taxed and used to fund and sustain custodial institutions designed to serve the ailing and the wayward. Perhaps Georgina Dopico Black puts it best when she describes the celebrated actress of public theatre as the "unrepentant *puta* whose profits ... benefit repentant ones" ("Public Bodies" 6). Thus women in early modern Spain stood at the centre of a complex spiritual and sexual economy where the wages of sin were used to pay for the rehabilitation or the containment of women or both. Public theatre was the newest player in this long-standing spiritual and sexual economy. Across southern Europe, funds generated for custodial institutions such as the magdalen house were traditionally collected through the taxation of such "sinful" arenas as liquor vendors, civic brothels, or fines for homosexuality.

In their earliest forms, custodial institutions had multiple functions; for example, the same space could act simultaneously as an orphanage and as a hospital. Although most custodial institutions operated as multiuse organizations until well into the eighteenth century, when specific populations and functions were more clearly defined, it is possible to trace a pervasive concern with the containment and correction of women throughout sixteenth- and seventeenth-century Spain.[9] During this long period, public theatres were also consolidated and professionalized. By the end of the sixteenth century, the general supervisor of the hospitals across the kingdom also controlled the *corrales* (public theatres). Although scholars of the period tend to focus on the decline of the Spanish empire and its concern with social control, paradoxically, these two centuries represent a time that Lisa Vollendorf has called the "foundational period for women's intellectual and educational history" (*Lives of Women* 3). Custodial institutions and their practices of rehabilitation reflected a paradox: on the one hand, strict control and punishment were central to many institutions; on the other hand, these same institutions at times provided better opportunities, greater protection, and enhanced education for both secular and religious women.[10]

Early modern custodial institutions for women were messy in form and function. Many were designed to benefit women's physical, spiritual, and economic well-being, instead of being oriented exclusively towards social control. As Michel Foucault makes clear, the rise in institutional projects exposes the way in which a state is disciplining itself and its subjects in new ways (although his focus was on France, Spain was no exception to this rule). Moreover, Foucault conceptualizes punishment as a complex social function and political tactic that exposes the interwoven concerns between penal law and human health. Yet, in terms of history, Foucault characterizes the early modern period as one dominated by the transparent and "horrifying spectacle of public punishment" (9) while the more encompassing form of punishment "at a distance, in the proper way, according to strict rules, and with a much 'higher' aim" (11) is not a real concept in his view until the late eighteenth century.

Public displays of punishment, religiosity, and penitence were a common fact of life in early modern Spain, especially in cities where the Inquisition's public *auto de fe* (act of faith) were performed. These dramatic acts of penitence and justice – consisting of the ritual of public penance of condemned heretics and the implementation of imposed sentences – were popular events in cities and attracted attention throughout Europe.[11] In the mid-sixteenth century a new set of rules for the ceremonial *auto de fe* was deliberately articulated by Inquisitor General Fernando de Valdés, in order to "stag[e] a flamboyant public ceremony that would reaffirm the power of the Inquisition and enforce its presence" (Kamen 205). The elaborate fanaticism of these spectacles has certainly coloured the history of the period, yet Henry Kamen reminds us that, "the popularity of public *autos* was in part a result of their comparative rarity ... virtually once-in-a-lifetime events" (212).[12] The phenomenon of the *auto de fe* may lead scholars to conclude that in Spain punishment and rehabilitation were predicated almost exclusively on visible, dramatic acts. Yet, it is worth considering how the *auto de fe*, along with other Inquisitional practices, also relied on diffuse, nuanced, and hidden manifestations of power to which Foucault alludes as a characteristically "modern" development.

Similarly, practices of women's rehabilitation in early modern Spain depended both on public and clandestine enactments of power. Even in the very popular and public performances of the *comedias*, women's punishment and rehabilitation are enacted in contradictory ways: occurring both on and off the stage, mimed and gestured but not always spoken. Although the *auto de fe* may have been a once-in-a-lifetime event, its masterful staging of penitence and punishment markedly impacted the culture of the period and led to the production of a variety of smaller, yet powerful dramatic scenes of conversion.

The ability to read this topic is indebted to a boom of scholarship over the last twenty years that has taken significant steps to reflect women's multifaceted roles in early modern Spanish society and to draw attention to the importance of their cultural production. Recent critical work assists the task of contextualizing these developments within Spain and persuasively illustrates the ways in which women battled for public and political attention, correcting the long-standing belief that women in early modern Spain led starkly isolated or domestic lives.[13] Most important, scholars have illuminated the numerous ways in which women took active, often formative roles both inside the home as daughters, sisters, wives, mothers, partners, and lovers (to men and women), as well as outside the home as nuns, healers, actresses, writers, and educators. *Unruly Women* contributes to this flourishing field of study with an in-depth analysis of the performance of women's deviance and the enactment of gender-specific punishment both onstage and offstage.

Public theatre was a hotly criticized affair in early modern Spain. Rife with raunchy dramatic content, plays were believed to incite bad behaviour and even illness among their impressionable audiences. As

Thomas O'Connor summarizes, "If such plays constituted the routine fare of theatergoers, so the traditionalists argued, the lessons to be learned from them would surely include rebellion against parental authority, rejection of time-honored church teachings on sexual morality, and an affective liberation of young people" (33). Repeated calls for the reformation of plays' contents speak to the social anxieties of the time and views regarding the exemplary function of public theatre. The prohibitions articulated by the *Reformación de comedias*, for example, stated "that lascivious and lewd things, dances, songs and swaying (*meneos*), and of bad example shall not be performed" (Cotarelo y Mori, *Bibliografia,* 626b). The idea of public theatre as an exemplary realm is further reinforced in debates that suggest *entremeses* (one-act interludes) instructed people about dangers to be avoided at all costs and were therefore useful to spectators, whereas the *bailes* (dances) and *músicas* (music) were considered frivolous and irresponsible.

When, in the face of moral and social convention, women were permitted to set foot on the Spanish stage, the question of public theatre's legitimacy ceased to be solely a moral issue involving dramatic content. On 18 November 1587 the Council of Castile granted permission for women to act under the following conditions: they had to be married and could not dress as men (an edict issued and repealed at least nine times throughout the sixteenth and seventeenth centuries, likely an indication that the ruling was consistently ignored); moreover, boys could no longer play female roles.[14] This order gave Spanish women greater latitude as actresses than they enjoyed elsewhere in Europe. In England and France, women could not appear on stage until the second half of the seventeenth century, while in Italy boys continued to play female roles until the 1630s.[15]

Moralists were all the more outraged when women were legally permitted to perform in this already contested forum, where they quickly composed nearly half of acting troupes. In 1623, for example, Padre Pedro Fomperosa y Quintana critiqued the indecency of the rehearsal process. He describes the following scene:

A las mujeres muchas veces se los leen los hombres, unas por no saber leer, otras por abreviar en este ejercicio con lo que han de tomar por memoria. Ensayan luego juntos, siéntanse promiscuamente, míranse y háblanse cara a cara sin reparo, ni nota, ni miedo. A estos ensayos, como son de cada día, es preciso estar las mujeres como de casa y medio desnudas.[16]

Often men will read to women, some because they can't read, others to shorten the exercise of what they must memorize. After they rehearse together, they promiscuously sit together, looking at each other, and talking face to face without objection, or note, or fear. At these rehearsals, as they take place daily, women must be as if they are at home and half-nude.[17]

As Fomperosa y Quintana describes, public theatre resembled an alternate and seriously perilous universe where actresses and actors freely intermingled in close quarters and in scanty dress, reading aloud and gazing unashamed into each other's eyes.[18] During rehearsals there were no police (*alguaciles*) to regulate behaviour as there were in performance. Although the conduct of both male and female actors was regarded as suspect, women's behaviour was regulated more heavily. Girls over the age of twelve needed to be accompanied by their father or husband, and men were not to be received in an actress's dressing room more than twice.

Sumptuary laws were particularly stringent for actresses. For example, women were not allowed to wear their costumes offstage. For leading actresses this was on the whole a strict code since their costumes were considered part of their personal property. Although their income was meagre, companies offset the wages of leading actors by including the ownership of costumes as part of their wages. Even after theatrical companies disbanded, it was common for actresses to receive a final payment for their services, frequently supplemented by costumes previously owned by the company (López Martínez 88–9). As Mary Blythe Daniels has argued, there was concern that the costumes could be used as "an entrapment for innocent males. Authorities tried to make these behavioural codes literal by passing laws which denied the actress access to her own wardrobe when she was on the street" (135).[19]

Speculation on the moral authority of the early modern Spanish actress extended well outside of her roles on stage. Increasingly stringent sumptuary laws that targeted women may be partially explained by the following example from Cotarelo y Mori. In this anecdote, the seductive quality of the actress and her wardrobe dangerously upset cherished divisions between classes:

Un titulado deste reino se enredó de tal manera de los amores de una mugercilla representante que no solamente le daba su hacienda, pero públicamente con notable escándalo de la República le tenía puesta casa

y vajilla de plata, le bordaban vestidos y la servían y respetaban sus cria-
dos como si fuera muger legítima, y aun la que lo era pasaba a esta causa
muchas descomodidades. Y llegó a tanta miseria este caballero que sufría
otros rivales infames ... que trataban con la mugercilla, solamente por ten-
erla contenta.

A titled man from this kingdom became so entangled with the love of this
lady actress that he not only gave her his estate, but to the considerable
scandal of the Republic, he publicly gave her his home and silverware,
embroidered her dresses, and had her served and respected by maids as if
she were a legitimate woman, and even she who was [legitimate – i.e., his
wife] suffered many calamities because of this. And this gentleman came
to such misery that he put up with other infamous rivals who had relations with his lady, just to keep her content. (*Bibliografía* 66)

The story reflects the widespread rumour that actresses were better po-
sitioned than other women to deceive men, especially men of a higher
social class.[20] Even worse, this story warns readers of how the actress is
allowed by her lovesick nobleman to pass for a reputable woman..
   Actresses were commonly criticized by moralists for their purpose-
ful disregard of rank and class, and were notorious for their real or
imagined extramarital affairs. Not only did actresses shun the guidance
of moral and behavioural norms offstage, but they were also regarded
with both suspicion and admiration for their chameleon-like ability to
play both saint and sinner on stage. In this context of suspicion, the
handful of cases in which actresses were recognized for their capacity
to be rehabilitated from the "evils" of the stage provides important information. Although we are still missing significant details about their
lives, it is worth considering the lives of early modern Spanish actresses
who converted to the religious life, including Eufrasia María de Reina,
Isabel Hernández, María Agueda, Josefa Lobaco, Francisca "La Baltasara" de los Reyes, María de Riquelme, Mariana Romero, and Teresa Escudo.[21] Each biography is significant as it illuminates a less studied side
of actresses' transformative power, as well as their formative relationship to the early modern church, which assisted them through various
aspects of conversion. Because actresses were commonly perceived to
be morally inferior to other women, tales of their successful conversion
would have been especially gratifying stories for contemporaries.
   Another prominent example can be found in the intriguing life of
the celebrated actress "La Calderona" (María Inés Calderón), who by

1643 became abbess of the Benedictine monastery of San Juan Bautista in Valfermoso de las Monjas. Daniels explains that the actress allegedly stopped a duel between her two lovers, the Duke of Medina de las Torres and King Philip IV, with her decision to enter the convent (157). A contemporary portrait of "La Calderona" titled *Alegoría de la Vanidad* (Allegory of Vanity) illustrates the contrast between the actress's two lives in compelling detail, representing an instructive allegory through side-by-side portraits.[22] On the left, "La Calderona" is depicted seated in an elegant chair, dressed in an ornate skirt and bodice, both trimmed with lace and pearls. Her cleavage is dramatically exposed as she adjusts a gold comb in her long auburn hair while staring directly at her audience. On the right, she is depicted in modest dress, kneeling and praying, eyes averted in the shadows. In stark contrast to the image on the left, her hair is pulled back and her head covered.[23] The dynamic relationship between these two figures makes clear reference to other popular images of conversion, particularly those featuring Mary Magdalene and her sister Martha, important in this context for the explicit connection it makes between the early modern actress and the prostitute.

The conversion stories of other actresses even inspired literary adaptations of their lives. For example, Vélez de Guevara co-wrote *La Baltasara* (1652) in honour of Francisca Baltasara de los Reyes (with Antonio Coello and Rojas Zorilla), celebrating her dramatic conversion from immoral actress to saintly woman.[24] In one memorable scene-within-a-scene, the actress cannot remember her own lines because she is so distracted by her newfound relationship with God. These stories of actresses' religious conversions were certainly not the norm. Yet they complement especially well the more conventional stage tales of women transformed or domesticated by marriage, while they also highlight the complexity of actresses' performances, which were commonly perceived to violate social convention.

The legal latitude extended to Spanish actresses temporarily came to an end as public theatres closed in 1646 in response to concerns about the morality of the plays' content and performance. According to O'Connor, Don Pedro Núñez de Guzmán explained in a 1672 letter to Queen Mariana that four arguments were advanced to reauthorize public theatre: first, the needs of the hospitals (who relied on the funds generated from the tax on theatre); second, the policy of entertaining the populace; third, the requirements of staging the Corpus Christi celebrations; and finally, dynastic interests, due to the celebration of the marriage of Felipe IV and Mariana de Austria (150). These four arguments succinctly convey the unique position of public theatre in early modern Spain and its intersections with the interests of church, court, and public welfare. Its celebrated heroines acted at once as the powerhouse behind charitable, Christian institutions of healing as well as the common well of diversion, laughter, and decadence. In sum, women stood at a complex intersection of pressing social preoccupations: the moral and pragmatic debates concerning the proper place and exemplary status of women; the regulation and staging of women's speech and bodies; and lastly, the economic and social interdependence between custodial institutions and public theatre as dramatic sites of rehabilitation.

This book is divided into two parts. The first part focuses on real-life sites of rehabilitation; the second part focuses on women onstage. The underlying themes of the two sections are the contradictory practices of punishment and penitence imposed on early modern Spanish women. Part One questions the context by which custodial institutions and the public theatre became interdependent and the methods by which they prescribed normative roles for women. It also explores how custodial institutions were shaped by their interdependent economic relationship with public theatre, since the creation and sustenance of these institutions relied on tax revenue generated from the "illicit" nature and public consumption of theatrical productions. To address these concerns, chapter 1, "Gendering *Recogimiento* in Early Modern Madrid," focuses on two of Madrid's most well-known yet understudied institutions: a magdalen house, La Casa de Santa María Magdalena de la Penitencia (founded 1587), and a harsher jail for women, *la galera* (founded circa 1608). Studies on the world of women's penitentiaries are few and very recent. Concepción Yagüe Olmos offers some context for this gap in scholarship, as she explains: "the arduous task of collecting historical documents joins an unavoidable difficulty: the almost total absence of references to women's prisons in the most famous manuals and articles" (5).[25] Yet through the study of lesser-known institutional manuals and legal documents, this section compares the distinct rehabilitative strategies employed by two representative custodial institutions and considers the ways in which these varied strategies, particularly the practice of *recogimiento*, utilize and adapt rehabilitative conventions made popular in the narratives of public theatre. The magdalen house, for example, often staged the rehabilitation of repentant prostitutes, and offered women the option of beginning life anew by entering either religious life or marriage. Alternatively, the *galera* aimed to offer deviant women "equality" through harsh corporeal and concealed punishments identical in severity to those experienced by their male counterparts.[26]

Following the overview of institutional responses to deviant female behaviour in early modern Spain, Part Two moves from the historical to the theatrical realm to consider in depth representations of the "unruly woman" on stage. It takes as a point of departure three representative yet distinct representations of female deviance: the widow, the vixen, and the murderess. Each of these unique and emblematic character types can be tied to a broader theme that concerns societal expectations for women. This study links the widow, the vixen, and the murderess to the topics of marriage, sex, and violence respectively, and explores as well the various connections among and between them. For all three archetypes, non-normative relationships to these important social topics are shown to require rehabilitation or punishment. Although each chapter analyses the archetype through a close reading of one particular *comedia*, I also offer evidence to prove that the character is not a singular example but rather speaks to broader trends within early modern Spanish theatre.

Chapter 2 turns to a figure that exemplifies the kind of witty defiance that makes the heroines of the Spanish *comedia* so memorable. "Stage Widow in Pedro Calderón de la Barca's *La dama duende*" focuses on the theatrical escapades of its widowed protagonist, Ángela. As unofficial playwright, stage architect, prop master, and actress, Ángela uses theatrical strategies to enable a romantic escapade with her love interest Don Manuel. Her innate dramatic prowess allows the young widow to pass within two important settings: the strict enclosure of the domestic sphere and the risks of Madrid's burgeoning city streets. Calderón's play offers to readers an extended meditation on widows' evolving relationships to the urban landscape, a concern that compels the play's action as well as its contemporary audiences. Although the theatre provides Ángela with fantastic freedoms, the play offers its own rehabilitative strategy when she is silenced and married at the conclusion. Wrapping up a narrative largely driven by Ángela's dramatic expertise, this moral and celebratory end is hardly the resolution it seems. By situating the analysis of the play in the context of historical records on widows and rehabilitation, this chapter explores how the comedy provides significant information about the status and treatment of young widows.

Chapter 3, "Dramatizing Women's Community in María de Zayas's *La traición en la amistad*," addresses the interplay among the protagonist's unkind behaviour, female community, and the *comedia* as an instructive tool. The play's heroine, Fenisa, is punished at the play's end for abandoning her female friends and disturbing an otherwise idyllic female community through her indiscreet romantic exploits. The chapter argues that Fenisa, her exploits, and the archetype of the vixen merit critical attention in order to illuminate the norms of the female community in which she participates. By exposing the ways in which the play both condemns and celebrates Fenisa as a figure in need of rehabilitation, the chapter explores an alternative representation of women's community and its norms. Because controlled circulation and containment of women's bodies was central to social order, as the example of the *galera* reveals, a complete account of women's relations can only be assembled when aberrance and deviation are also included.

While the previous chapter outlines the status of an exemplary model of women's community, the final chapter, "Women's Exemplary Violence in Luis Vélez de Guevara's *La serrana de la Vera*," examines the exemplarity of a violent protagonist, Gila, who embodies at once model and villain. For Vélez de Guevara's audience this figure was doubly significant because the role of Gila was written for and played by one of the generation's most prominent actresses, Jusepa Vaca. By reading *La serrana de la Vera* through the lens of exemplarity, this chapter explores the ways in which the author achieves a moralizing effect through the display of Gila's violence, and the way this effect is mediated by the latitude extended to the early modern actress. Although contemporary norms demanded the containment of the female body, Vélez de Guevara's *comedia* takes the display of the actress to a new extreme. In her murderous rampage, the protagonist kills two thousand men. As punishment for her crimes, she is publicly executed at the order of Fernando and Isabel in order to serve as an example to other women. Pushing the limits of the unruly woman on stage, with a case where rehabilitation is no longer a viable solution, this chapter investigates the play's relationship to contemporary concerns, including the relationship between violence and women, and the contradictory moral lessons it offers.

By exploring the women in real-life rehabilitative institutions as well as the fictional depictions of women in the *comedia*, this book considers the ways in which these two separate spheres developed in close correspondence with one another. Each of these plays provocatively stages women behaving badly by casting its heroine in direct opposition to the social norms of the period. A consideration of these models and the popular responses they elicit informs the discussion of women's rehabilitation in early modern Spain, and offers contextualization for these concerns in the *comedia* as well as in contemporary custodial institutions. While the book separates institutional histories from fictional acts of the *comedia*, the links between these two spheres provide a means for interpreting the construction of social norms in early modern Spain. An advantage of this study's comparative nature is to demonstrate the ways dramatic texts engaged with real acts and historical concerns and how La Casa de Santa María Magdalena de la Penitencia and Madre Magdalena's *galera* were also deeply invested in the performative aspects of rehabilitation. Likewise, each play offers a distinct rehabilitative solution in response to its protagonist's unruly behaviour, ranging in severity from marriage to social exclusion, or even death.

Unruly Women puts into dialogue scenes of rehabilitation crafted by early modern Spanish dramatists alongside those staged by contemporary custodial institutions. Although historical evidence shows the two spheres were likely already informed by one another throughout the early modern period and beyond, this project takes significant steps to document their fascinating interrelationship, especially as it illuminates the obscured history of women's rehabilitation and the anxiety-ridden relationship between sexuality and entertainment. By examining the figure of the unruly woman, I argue that she is not merely a stock figure but rather that she dramatizes pressing and controversial issues for sixteenth- and seventeenth-century Spain: the rapidly changing role of women and the increased bureaucratization of the state, which was manifested in the creation of custodial institutions for women.

The rehabilitation exerted by these institutions acted as a contradictory yet commonplace practice of disciplinary containment and charitable protection. Accordingly, women, through performance and rehabilitation, negotiate with the dominant desire of the patriarchal system in which women are paradoxically constructed as at once defective and prized subjects. The negotiation also reveals the interconnected relationship between women's rehabilitation and the performance of penitence and punishment in the early modern period, while opening a space to imagine conflicting representations of women's increasing authority, onstage and off. Women's power was asserted in a variety of compelling forms vis-à-vis the display of the unruly woman. On the real-life and fictional stages of the period, she obediently fulfilled and assertively challenged the patriarchal desire of rehabilitation predicated on female submission and exposed the fear of women's changing roles in an increasingly urban landscape.

PART ONE

1
Gendering *Recogimiento* in Early Modern Madrid

One of the earliest and most prominent examples of public rehabilitation for women occurred in 1623, when the magdalen house, the Casa de Santa María Magdalena de la Penitencia (founded in 1587), relocated to a larger space and marched its charges in a solemn procession through the streets of Madrid.

> Llevároslas en Procesión, y pasároslas por el Monasterio de las Señoras Descalzas Reales, donde estaban los Reyes para verlas: allí cantaron todas una Salve, y al decir la Oración se postraron en tierra; cuyo acto causó mucha devoción. Iban de dos en dos, vestidas con un saco de sayal blanquecino ceñido, y un paño blanco, ó antifaz por encima del rostro, y con este orden llegaron al nuevo Recogimiento.

> They brought them in procession and had them pass the Monasterio de las Señoras Descalzas Reales, where the kings were waiting to see them; there they all sang a prayer while prostrating themselves on the ground, an act that inspired much devotion. They went two by two, dressed in a white fitted sackcloth robe, and a white wool cloth, or mask, covering their faces, and in this way they arrived at the new Recogimiento. (Recio 8–9)

Rehabilitation in the early modern period took many forms including prayer, marriage, work, and corporal punishment. In this example, like a troupe of actors enacting street theatre, the repentant prostitutes were paraded before crowds throughout the city streets, even granted audience by the king and queen. With prayerful prostration and public singing, the simple act of moving from one building to another offered this magdalen house the opportunity for an exemplary performance, both pious and shameful. Dressed in white with covered faces, these figures inevitably evoke parallel exemplary scenes well known from the Spanish comedies. When Lope de Vega, for example, describes the punishment levied on the unfaithful wife in *El castigo sin venganza* (Punishment without Revenge) (1631), he writes: "La infame Casandra dejo / de pies y manos atada, / con un tafetán cubierta" (He left the infamous Casandra with hands and feet tied, and a taffeta cover) (2858–60). While the two scenes vary significantly in tone – the first a pious celebration, the second a moralizing tragedy – both utilize parallel material references in order to create an exemplary scene, in which private acts of penance are meticulously staged in public settings.

Like the numerous public displays of punishment, religiosity, and penitence staged during the period, especially those in cities where the *auto de fe* took place, the magdalen house projected a calculated image of its purpose and practices to onlookers in Madrid. Dependence on public spectacle as an exemplary technique was not unique to La Casa de Santa María Magdalena de la Penitencia; rather, it was a common practice employed by most contemporary magdalen houses. Clerics frequently partnered with the administrators of brothels to deliver special public sermons to groups of prostitutes on the feast day of Mary Magdalene. The goal of the sermon was to elicit public conversion, often celebrated by a group processional from the brothel to the cathedral. As Teófilo F. Ruiz astutely reminds readers in his 2012 study on the role of festivals in late medieval and early modern Spain, "Displays were exaggerated ... But representations also tell us important things about the nature of society, about the men and women who participated in these festive events, who gazed upon them and upon each other, who paid for them, and who scripted them for the benefit of those in power, those seeking power, or those contesting power" (11). Public corporal punishment of prostitutes was also typical; as Cruz and Perry explain, "Traditional regulations required these Jezebels to be punished through public humiliation, whippings, having their nostrils slit, and exile" (141). This conflation between penitence and punishment was more visibly popularized in the period by the inquisitional *auto de fe*.

The procession described above parallels the new set of rules for the *auto* crafted by the Inquisitor General Fernando de Valdés in 1561, where the presence and patronage of the royal court gave the ceremony prestige. For example, Kamen describes how prisoners from Galicia and Andalusia were brought to Madrid in a 1680 *auto* in the city's Plaza Mayor, "to make the holding of an *auto* worthwhile"; the date for the scene was set more than a month prior to the ceremony, preparations were elaborate, and a procession like the one described above – replete with public processions, sung prayer, and royal audience – was held for prisoners as they were brought into the public square where the *auto* took place (Kamen 206–7).[1] Although the magdalen house and the inquisitional practice of the *auto* shared a common investment in public enactments of the power of exemplary rehabilitation, the mission statement of La Casa de Santa María Magdalena de la Penitencia shows how the magdalen house also relied on other multifaceted deployments of *recogimiento*:

> Viven las Hermanas en este retiro con grande *recogimiento*, en continuo ejercicio de oración, penitencia, y mortificación, de suerte que si con la vida pasada escandalizaron la República, después la edifican con su *ejemplo*.

> The sisters live in this retreat with great *recogimiento*, in continuous exercise of prayer, penitence, and mortification, so that if in a past life they threatened the Republic, they later help build it with their *example*. (Recio 13, emphasis mine)

Recogimiento, the idea of gathering up or gathering within, can be viewed as a theological concept, a virtue, and an institutional practice.[2] First developed in the late fifteenth and early sixteenth centuries by Castilian mystics as a practice of physical isolation or enclosure, or a meditation on "nothing" in order to deny self and unite with God, the word *recogimiento* can be used in nominal, adjectival, and verb form. *Recogimiento* can also be understood as a gendered practice of modesty and controlled behaviour, most frequently applied to women's bodies and sexuality.[3] As Sebastián de Covarrubias's 1611 *Tesoro de la lengua castellana o española* clearly indicates, during the early modern period the word *recogimiento* was linked to a constellation of interrelated terms including the noun *retiramiento* as well as the verbs *recoger, ayuntar, retirarse,* and *coger*. According to Covarrubias, *recogimiento* implies a solitary, meditative experience – "recoger es recibir en sí alguna cosa" (*recoger* is to receive something in one's self) – as well as the following divergent definitions: "Decimos: 1. coger los frutos de la tierra, 2. coger al ladrón, prenderle" (We say: 1. gather the fruits of the earth, 2. catch the thief, arrest him) (329). The word signifies a number of contradictory practices, including receiving, punishing, and harvesting.

These multiple definitions of *recogimiento* seamlessly link women's spiritual needs (interiority, meditation, and recollection) with contemporary social and political concerns (detaining, ordering, and confining). Institutions designed in the name of spiritual and physical wellness would often fulfil a variety of other social and political concerns, in particular the control of women's bodies and their sexuality. As the case of the Casa de Santa María Magdalena de la Penitencia demonstrates, *recogimiento* also has an exemplary function, especially as it relates to social and political goals. As an institutional practice, numerous girls and women participated in *recogimiento*, willingly or unwillingly, in a variety of custodial institutions. These institutions, which include places as varied as magdalen houses, *beaterios*, orphanages, hospitals, and jails, gained popularity in the early sixteenth century, and were later revitalized as part of Counter Reformation projects designed to remediate persons considered to be either sickly or defective members of society.[4] As Vollendorf attests, "Conversion houses offered a legitimate space for controlling women" (*Lives* 93). These multiple definitions of *recogimiento* thus allowed for the creation of institutional spaces for women with complex and sometimes contradictory functions.

The Spanish Inquisition produced an exceptionally stringent moral and social "norm," regulated by questions of honour and purity of blood (i.e., all-Christian blood), and enforced through expulsion from Spain or even death.[5] While Jews and Muslims were the most conspicuous symbols of the need for conversion, women too – especially "fallen women," ambiguously defined – stood out as visible figures in need of rehabilitation. Not surprisingly, abandoned, disabled, or abused wives and daughters, as well as unwed mothers, were among those most affected by Spain's economic crisis.[6] As the Counter Reformation in Spain was mobilized by means of royal decrees designed to cleanse and order urban spaces, a focus on housing and rehabilitating women emerged.[7]

Throughout the early modern period, the prevalence of accusations and legible penalization of women in relation to their moral and sexual character (*irreverencia, moral, sexual, fautoría, impureza, excesos, bigamia, adulterio*) was second only to accusations and penalizations in relation to the practice of, or association with, a prohibited religion (*islamismo, judaísmo, irreligiosidad*).[8] In Granada, for example, María Isabel Pérez de Colosía Rodríguez explains that women were more frequently accused of religious violations since they were entrusted with rituals and practices as part of their domestic education so they would be able to instruct their children and preserve family traditions ("Mujeres" 425). She explains that in many cases women practised these rituals without any knowledge of their religious meaning (lighting two candles on

Friday evening, for example), yet were still accused of associating with a prohibited religion (the Jewish observance of Sabbath). Women were also punished for crimes of excessive spirituality or supernatural qualities (*conducta sospechosa, hechicería, superstición, visionaria*), as well as infanticide, abandonment, theft, and murder (*infanticidio, secuestro, robo, los castigos por fugas*).[9] It was common for those who were not closely allied with a family unit, that is, under the care of a father, brother, or husband, to be particularly suspect, although association with male care did not ensure any kind of guaranteed protection.[10]

In her study on the discourse of poverty and its relief through social reform in early modern Spain, Anne Cruz cites sixteenth- and seventeenth-century Spain's economic crisis and such interrelated factors as the lack of employment, heavy taxation, devaluation of money, and rise in prices as chiefly responsible for the rise in these kinds of reform projects.[11] She explains, the "economic crisis ... had been dealt with principally as a moral problem, and its accepted solution, charity, was religiously inspired" (*Discourses* 40). In other words, the troubles produced by the economic crisis were redressed and dealt with as moral concerns. This was true in Spain and across Europe throughout the early modern period; Gabriel Lance Lazar describes how new models were created for the roles and responsibilities of the individual, church, and state, where "cultural and institutional identity [was] based on new practices of faith" (3).

Madrid in particular experienced the bulk of its growth as a new capital during the reigns of Felipe II and Felipe III. David Ringrose explains that because it was a city that offered economic opportunities, the population nearly doubled between the years 1560 and 1625 and nearly three quarters of its inhabitants were immigrants (196).[12] During this same period, the city's internal system of plazas and adjoining streets was established. This division between plaza and street created several central spaces for public performance, often used to reaffirm the social and political order established by the court.[13] For example, Ringrose cites the Monasterio de San Jerónimo, the Puerta del Sol, the Plaza Mayor, and the Real Alcázar as the most important spaces of urban traffic during this period (180). Under Felipe IV, the new city map was even more firmly established:

Ese espacio urbano así absorbido fue entonces transformado con afirmaciones monumentales ... sobre la autoridad y la sociedad. Aquellas reconstrucciones pasajeras objetivaban a su vez el mundo imaginario

de la ideología dominante, sirviéndose del escenario urbano y las rutas
ceremoniales.

Thus absorbed, the urban space was transformed with monumental af-
firmations ... on authority and society. These transient reconstructions in
turn objectified the imaginary world of the dominant ideology, making
use of the urban landscape and ceremonial routes. (184)

This dramatic reconstruction of Madrid as urban capital had a significant impact on the lives of this city's residents. If public spaces were
designed primarily to reflect the power and order of the court, it is easy
to explain why such "street cleaning" projects flourished in the period.
Paradoxically, practices of *recogimiento* produced at least for a time
what Cruz describes as "a division of external and internal space for
women along behavioral lines – the 'good' women were literally locked
indoors, while the 'bad' had the run of the outdoors" (*Discourses* 140).
    This "bad" woman on the street calls to mind, of course, one of
the most notorious figures of the period: the female prostitute. Prostitution was a legal profession in early modern Spain, as it was believed that institutionalized brothels protected the health of marriage.
Yet prostitutes were perceived as outlaws for their sexual deviance
as well as their supposed economic independence. With syphilis on
the rise throughout the sixteenth-century Iberian Peninsula, Perry explains, moralists began to question the idea that legalized prostitution was a necessary evil: "They found in prostitution a commercial
prop, an agency to reinforce lines of authority, and a symbol of evil.
They pointed to prostitutes as diseased, disgusting, and parasitical.
Prostitution became a symbol that united the community and justified the extension of governmental powers" (*Crime and Society* 212).[14]
As ideas about the utility of prostitution began to change, so too did
ideas concerning the proper place of prostitutes, both active and no
longer working. If they were to leave the brothel by choice or by force,
most agreed they should be placed "in another form of enclosure"
(Cruz and Perry, *Culture* 131). Custodial institutions used the closed
and controlled space that had appealed to state and church authorities in relation to brothels, but the mission and practice of these institutions reflected a changing morality.
    I turn now to the institutional and spiritual practices of *recogimiento*
as the key rehabilitative practice exercised by two of Madrid's best-
known, yet understudied, custodial institutions. The first is a traditional

magdalen house, the Casa de Santa María Magdalena de la Penitencia (founded in 1587), a religious order founded on the cult of Mary Magdalene and dedicated to the reform and redemption of prostitutes.[15] The second is Madre Magdalena de San Jerónimo's *galera* (founded circa 1608), a harsher jail designed as a model of penal reform that responded directly to deficiencies perceived in the magdalen house model.[16] Both the magdalen house and the *galera* have a complex institutional history. Their organizations, missions, and even their names changed repeatedly throughout the late sixteenth and early seventeenth centuries.

By exploring both the public and private enactments of *recogimiento* employed by these two institutions, I explore the gendered dynamics of this spiritual and rehabilitative practice. As the procession enacted by the magdalen house at the start of this section reminds us, there are a number of related issues to explore: the exemplarity of public performances as both an instructive and perilous strategy, the gendering of spirituality and punishment, questions of authorship and audience, as well as the intersection of moral and economic concerns, especially as they relate to the control of women. Although Foucault has firmly situated the early modern practice of public punishment or rehabilitation as a deterrent to criminality, the custodial institutions I discuss are distinctive because of their gender segregation, the rehabilitation and punishment of moral infractions as well as criminal acts, as well as their explicit braiding of religious, judicial, and penal discourses.

I Reforming Prostitutes: Madrid's Magdalen House

As María Dolores Pérez Baltasar points out, the Casa de Santa María Magdalena de la Penitencia was one of the best-known magdalen houses in Madrid. By 1601 it was popularly referred to as Las Recogidas de Madrid, which again demonstrates the complexities of *recogimiento* as both a spiritual and punitive practice of rehabilitation. Don Manuel Recio authored its institutional manual in 1777 in Madrid. Titled *Compendio histórico, y manifiesto instructivo del origen, y fundación de la Real Casa de Santa María Magdalena de la Penitencia, vulgo las Recogidas de Madrid*, the work had a double function, as both the first recorded institutional history and as a guidebook for the current institution.

Recio was the *Oficial* of the General Accounting of the Royal Granery (Oficial de la Contaduría general de Pósitos del Reyno) and at the time of writing the manual, he was the archivist of La Real Hermandad de María Santísima de la Esperanza, the eighteenth-century administrators of the magdalen house. As Recio explains in his introduction, his history is the first and most comprehensive of the magdalen house: "tiene la recomendación de la primera noticia formal, y cierta, que se ha escrito del origen, fundación y circunstancias de la Real Casa" (it has the recommendation of being the first formal and true work to write on the origin, foundation, and circumstances of the *Real Casa*) (3). The fact that Recio writes this history and institutional manual for the institution well over one hundred years after it was originally founded provides an interesting framework from which to discuss the eighteenth-century perspective on women's rehabilitation.[17]

Recio writes that the house served women who had been labelled as "públicas pecadoras" (public sinners) and would only release them under two conditions: either as "Religiosa" (Religious) or "Casada" (Married) (196). He explains this:

> Como el santo instituto de la casa era dirigido a recoger en ella aquellas mujeres, que habían vivido licenciosamente, y que tocadas de la poderosa mano de Dios, se retiraban allí a hacer seria penitencia de los excesos a que las había conducido su libertad; se las dieron reglas, y estatutos muy prudentes, y apropiadas a este intento, atendiendo también en ellas a las fuerzas, salud, y complexión de las tales mujeres.

> As the holy mission of the house was designed to *recoger* these women, who had lived licentiously, and who, touched by the powerful hand of God, retired to this house to do penitence for the excesses to which their freedoms had led them, they were given rules and very prudent statutes, and ones appropriate for this purpose, attending also to the health, strength, and build of these women. (6)

The use of *recoger* in this fragment emphasizes the conflicting institutional mission as a space of both punitive containment and spiritual retreat. Since women could only be released from the magdalen house as religious or married women, the house invested significantly in the inhabitants in order to facilitate this requirement. In addition to offering a religious and domestic education, many of these institutions provided to women the advantage of a dowry upon marriage. In this way Recio depicts *recogimiento* as an advantageous practice for women, both financially and socially: "uno de los laudables Estatutos de la Hermandad era el recoger, mantener, y sustentar mugeres, que su fragilidad las hubiese hecho incurrir en culpa, dirigiendo a unas para voluntario perpetuo recogimiento, y a otras para conducirlas a sus patrias con sus padres, o parientes" (one of the laudable Statutes of this Hermandad was to *recoger*, maintain, and support women, whose fragility had led them to fault, directing some to voluntary and perpetual *recogimiento*, and others to their homes with their parents or other relatives) (114). As he cites their naturally weak moral character, Recio positions women at the centre of sexual and spiritual interchange where women are saved from their own natural defects through placement under the guardianship of either church or family. According to the author, women are in a unique position to require this kind of moral guidance.

Prior to operating as a magdalen house, the space first housed the well-known Hospital de Peregrinos, which offered lodging and meals to pilgrims and other travellers. The hospital was founded by a Franciscan tertiary, Madrid's Orden tercera de San Francisco, in partnership with the confraternity of Nuestra Señora de la Gracia in 1555. The hospital's location was made possible by the gift of Doña Ana Rodríguez, who donated her property for the purpose of opening the hospital. Doña Ana's charitable contribution is important because it offers yet another example of a woman actively participating in and contributing to the creation of custodial institutions, although her original donation was not meant for a female-only space, but rather had a broad focus on charitable works as a pious practice. She is referred to by the nineteenth-century historian Antonio Capmany y Montopaulau as "una virtuosa viuda" (a virtuous widow) (326) because her charitable acts mitigate her otherwise perilous status as widow, a topic that will be explored in more detail in the following chapter.

In 1580 the hospital was restructured and incorporated the sponsorship of a second confraternity, La Cofradía de la Vera-Cruz, in order to cater to the growing needs of a larger population. In 1601 the hospital was redesigned for a third time, and this time focused exclusively on women. Each of these three reorganizations reflected the changing social concerns of the period. Most of the female residents originated from their protection under the order of Las religiosas agustinas de la Magdalena. According to Jerónimo de la Quintana, they entered into the house on their own volition although the nuns may have been ordered to move: "dejando la ocasión de culpa se querían retirar y entregar con veras al servicio de Nuestro Señor" (left the occasion of sinning in order to retire and dedicate themselves to the service of our Lord).[18]

At the start of the seventeenth century these *arrepentidas* (repentant women) occupied only a fraction of the complex and were closely supervised by two or three nuns. By the end of the century, the casa revolved around its *recogimiento* practices and served close to forty women. Women who were able were required to donate one hundred ducats in order to enter the house; others were taken in without cost. The case to fund magdalen houses was easily made as a charitable enterprise, designed to protect women from their naturally "defective" status and preserve the health of the larger community. Under the Royal Patronage of 1618, the Casa de Santa María Magdalena de la Penitencia was protected under the name of Don Francisco de Contreras, a member of the council of Castile, the supernumerary representative of the Confraternity of the Soledad, and general supervisor of the hospitals (Recio 5). Contreras's protection is important because, according to Varey and Davis's records, institutions under his patronage were funded, at least in part, by revenue generated from public theatres and their celebrated actresses (*Los corrales 1574–1615* 22, 38, 154, 159). In this way it is possible to explicitly link the financial welfare of the magdalen house with the stability of its contemporary public theatres.

The scene of rehabilitation at the start of this chapter emphasizes the public and exemplary function of *recogimiento*. Parallel techniques, involving the careful staging of the women's bodies, were also used as a rehabilitative strategy behind closed doors. *Recogimiento* can thus be read as both a public and private practice. An overview of daily life within the Casa de Santa María Magdalena de la Penitencia further affirms the keen awareness of appearance as a powerful tool for rehabilitation. On a daily basis, women were to be dressed in "honest" colours and closed-toed shoes "sin curiosidad, ni tacones" (without fanciful things, nor high heels) (Recio 196). Private spaces were clearly defined and closely monitored. Women, for example, were not permitted to share beds and were punished for attempting to sleep together, sing, dance, or gossip.[19] As was typical of the austere magdalen house, daily routines revolved around strict regimens of work and prayer. Clear hierarchies of power were established, with at least nine people in supervisory positions. Women were publicly disciplined according to the degree of their transgressions. For example, to compensate for a moderate transgression, a woman would have to eat sitting on the floor instead of at the table on Fridays over two months and kiss everyone's feet before and after each meal. Provisions were also in place to prevent residents from forming friendships (which could cause jealousy or spark concerns about same-sex relations). Anyone found guilty of these relationships was punished with "disciplina de rueda" (cudgeling) (Recio 25).

As the charges of the Casa de Santa María Magdalena made their debut as repentant women, they were dressed in new robes, escorted into the church, received by the confessor, and immediately led to prayer at the main altar of the sanctuary. Since these details correspond so closely to the monastic rite of reception, the ceremony suggests that the former prostitute was passing from one state of fallen secular life into a religious one:

> Se la entrega una efigie de Cristo crucificado, y con ella en los brazos se la conduce por la puerta que desde la Iglesia entra a la clausura de la Casa, en donde está la Comunidad formada, con sus velos, o antifaces, velas encendidas, cruz, y ciriales para recibirla; y cantando el *Te Deum*, la llevan en procesión al Coro bajo; y dichas las demás oraciones, y bendiciones, que se acostumbran en semejantes casos, la desnudan allí del vestido seglar de gala, y se la viste el hábito, con otras ceremonias de mucha devoción, y ternura.

> She is given an effigy of the crucified Christ, and with it in her arms she is led to the door in the church that opens into the cloister of the house, where the Community is assembled with their veils or masks, lit candles, cross, and candle holders to receive her; and singing the *Te Deum*, she is led in procession to the lower choir; and saying other prayers and blessings, as is customary in these cases, she is undressed from her lay robes and is dressed in the habit, with other very devoted and tender ceremonies. (Recio 193)

The re-dressing of the former prostitute is strongly suggestive of the vesting of a nun in the order of reception as novices into a religious order. By giving an effigy of the crucified Christ to the initiate, the ceremony powerfully signifies the replacing of the sinful sexual body of male patrons with that of the suffering body of Christ. It is likewise suggestive that the effigy is described as being "in her arms," a kind of affectionate embrace. When the former prostitute is "undressed from her lay robes," which strongly evokes what she has been doing in a carnal context, and then re-dressed in the "habit," the ceremony again visually indicates a spiritual transformation and reception into a new life. As the former prostitute formally takes her position as a repentant woman, rehabilitative rituals are mediated by a relationship to audience and performance. The magdalen house relied on displays of rehabilitation – both public and private – in order to promote changed behaviour within its own walls as well as to project an image of successful rehabilitation to its outside audience and patrons.

II Reforming the Magdalen House: Madre Magdalena de San Jerónimo's *galera*

In 1608 the nun Madre Magdalena de San Jerónimo proposed the creation of a prison, or *galera*, exclusively for Spanish women, which would employ novel forms of discipline and punishment that mimicked existing disciplinary systems designed for men. The proposal based its recommendations on her experience directing one of Valladolid's magdalen houses, the Casa Pía de Arrepentidas de Santa Magdalena (founded circa 1604). Although little is known about Madre Magdalena's personal life, it is recognized that she actively corresponded with the infanta Isabel Clara Eugenia de Austria (1566–1633, daughter of Isabel de Valois and Felipe II) and the renowned mystic Luisa de Carvajal y Mendoza (1566–1614). In the service of the infanta (or perhaps her father), Madre Magdalena also travelled to England, Brussels, Paris, and Flanders where she acquired relics to donate to the city of Valladolid in favour of her Casa Pía, including at least twenty heads and two bodies of the eleven thousand virgins who accompanied St Ursula to martyrdom.[20] Barbeito Carniero explains that during her travels the nun met with a number of other accomplished, elite Spanish women, including the Carmelite nun Ana de Jesús and Madre Mariana de San José, the incoming prioress of the Royal Monastery of the Incarnation whom Madre Magdalena accompanied on her move to Madrid (*Cárceles* 40–1).[21] Her secular name may have been Beatriz Zamudio; whether it was or not, she likely belonged to the order of St Bernard and the house of Zamudio (*Cárceles* 37). Dopico Black also speculates that Madre Magdalena could have been a Magdalen herself ("Public Bodies" 81).

In her proposal *Razón y forma de la galera y casa real* (Reason and Form of the Galera and Royal House) (1608), Madre Magdalena petitioned King Felipe III to create a prison for women in Madrid defined by a regimen of reclusion and hardship. Her work is the first extant and exhaustive manual dedicated to the topic of a women's penitentiary and was indeed persuasive as Felipe III implemented her plan and called her to direct the *galera* in Madrid.[22] Other jails for women based on the *galera* model, what Almeda names the *casas galera*, were constructed in Valladolid, Zaragoza, Salamanca, Barcelona, Valencia, and Granada shortly afterwards ("Pasado" 78). The proposal offers a unique account of prison-based rehabilitation for women by a woman who had concrete experience implementing other models of rehabilitation for women. Rather than offer purely moral or religious speculation on the ills of society, Madre Magdalena relied on her administrative background with the successes and failures of magdalen houses in order to argue for the creation of the *galera*.

Madre Magdalena's strategic reliance on her own experience can be found, for example, when she employs the first person in her account: "Y esto sélo yo, porque muchas de las que he recogido me han dicho que se habían perdido por causa de estas malas madres, que mejor se podían llamar madrastras y echar y remar su vida en esta Galera" (And this I know myself, because many of those that I have *recogido* have told me that they were lost as a result of these bad mothers, that could better be called stepmothers and placed to row their life away in this *galera*) (San Jerónimo 75–6).[23] Similarly, Madre Magdalena claims her experience with the *galera* allows her to testify to its effectiveness: "Y esto mismo se ha visto ahora en Madrid después que asentó la Galera" (I myself have seen this here in Madrid after they set up the *galera*) (90). The proposal offers readers a document of persuasion in favour of the jail model, as well as an evidence-based testimony on existing practices of women's rehabilitation. In addition, the proposal provides a unique account of a woman's perspective on rehabilitation as a practice that is more effective when directed to the specific needs of women.

While the majority of early modern Madrid's institutional norms were authored and endorsed by men, the proposal and subsequent creation of the *galera* provides scholars with the opportunity to study the roles of female authorship and endorsements as they relate to gender-specific rehabilitation. An acutely relevant example can be found in the fact that support for Madre Magdalena's *galera* repeatedly came in the form of correspondence, authored by a powerful community of women that included her friends the infanta Isabel Clara Eugenia de Austria and Luisa de Carvajal y Mendoza.[24] In a 1606 letter to the Count-Duke Olivares, for example, the infanta plainly advocates for Madre Magdalena de San Jerónimo's cause. She writes: "También escribo a mi hermano sobre la casa de Magdalena de San Jerónimo, a que os pido mucho que ayudeis, porque no se pierda aquella buena obra, y ella no falte en otras que acá trae entre manos" (I also write to my brother about the house of Madre Magdalena de San Jerónimo, which I ask that you help, so that this good project is not wasted and so that she does not fail in others in which she is engaged) (147). The infanta boldly steps outside of her traditional role and requests financial and political support in order to advocate for her ally through the use of letters.

Like the infanta, Madre Magdalena de San Jerónimo also employed the tools of epistolary negotiation as a way to bolster her own cause without overstepping her social role. In a letter to King Felipe III, for example, Madre Magdalena defended herself against not only those who criticized the severity of her proposal, but in particular those who were surprised that a woman could be so harsh to other women:

> Como las demás cosas nuevas en sus principios, así ésta ha causado novedad y admiración, no solo en la gente vulgar y común, pero aun en la principal, y más grave, teniendo el nombre y hechos de esta Galera por demasiado rigor y severidad, particularmente siendo inventada por *muger contra muger.*

> Just like other new things at their start, this one has aroused novelty and admiration, not only among the vulgar and common people, but even among the prominent; and more seriously, considering the name and acts of this *galera* too rigorous and severe, particularly as it was invented by a *woman against women.* (65–6, emphasis mine)

Madre Magdalena's explanation reveals the tenuous position of women, obligated to protect the norms of their community while maintaining a docile and affable appearance. Despite the fact that her proposal fits squarely in line with the humanist rhetoric of her period (in which men and women were required to police and isolate those who assaulted or offended their sex), at the same time it is necessary to emphasize how, as a woman, the author is subject to preserving an adequately "feminine" appearance. Madre Magdalena stands out as an anomalous figure because she argues for equitable punishment between men and women: "Yo, absolutamente, no quiero el rigor; pero, supuesta la herida, es menester cura que duela" (I, absolutely, do not want rigour; but, assuming the injury, the necessary cure hurts) (94). Although she situates herself as opposed to the rigour commonly known to characterize penal institutions for men, she ultimately argues that it is an effective form of punishment that women also deserve.[25] All the while, in a cautionary and rather strategic move, she emphasizes her ongoing protection from King Felipe III, even referencing his early enthusiasm for her work four years prior to the proposal.[26]

The *galera* was designed not only to remedy the moral and behavioural ills of deviant women but also to act as a corrective to other social welfare institutions for women. Based on her experience as administrator of the magdalen house, Madre Magdalena argued that these institutions no longer achieved their goals because many women required stricter punishment than was offered. By designing a place for the "worst" kind of women, Madre Magdalena believed that other institutions would be better able to meet the needs of their residents. The target population of the *galera* was the most broad-ranging and ambitious to date, with aims to remediate women who were excessively sexual, destitute, sickly, or otherwise considered dangerous. Since the *galera* acted as a corrective to less rigid social welfare institutions, it also initiated a significant conversation on the different forms of rehabilitation possible for women. As another example of a court-funded project designed to conceal deviant behaviour, the project also reflects Madrid's changing urban landscape and its increased concerns with projecting cleanliness and order.

Women were commonly housed in the *galera* from fifteen days to a year, depending on the gravity of their crimes and their responsiveness to the institutional programming.[27] The *galera* was run by five principal administrators, which included a minister whose main job was to find and seize or *recoger* women: "buscar y prender todas las mujeres que toparen de noche por las esquinas, cantones, portales, caballerizas y otras partes semejantes; y de día en las casas donde se dan las limosnas" (find and detain all of the women whom they [the administrators] encounter at night on street corners, doorsteps, stables, and other similar places, and during the day go out to beg for charity) (San Jerónimo 83–4). While this process of detaining women appears to be a strictly punitive action, the *galera* obtained significant monetary benefits from the use of its inmates as workers.[28] The *galera* struggled to secure consistent funding, and relied heavily on city funds and private charity. According to Leonardo Galdiano y Croy, the *galera*'s total income in 1676 was 954 ducats, severely short of their total operating expense of 1,936 ducats (41). This difficult financial situation likewise limited the number of those admitted to the *galera* to approximately seventy or eighty. As Pike explains, "in 1676 there were only fifty-nine women in the *galera*, and they were living in conditions of extreme poverty and want, a situation that continued to characterize this establishment through the eighteenth century" (6).

Madre Magdalena's proposal is divided into five major sections: "De la importancia y necesidad de esta Galera" (On the importance and necessity of this *Galera*); "De la forma y traza de ella" (On the form and appearance of it); "Los avisos para la justicia y para los ministros de la Galera" (Notes for the Justice and Ministers of the *Galera*); "De los provechos que de ella se siguen" (On the benefits brought by it); and

"Una exhortación a los jueces y gobernadores de la república" (An exhortation to the judges and governors of the Republic). The proposal's subtitle – "Que el rey, nuestro señor, manda hacer en estos reinos, para castigo de las mujeres vagantes, y ladronas, alcahuetas, hechiceras, y otras semejantes" (That the king, our lord, orders to be made in this kingdom, for the punishment of vagrant women, thieves, go-betweens, and sorceresses, and other similar women) – speaks to the breadth of the institution's population as the *galera* was designed to punish bad women, broadly defined. The nun carefully demarcates between deviant women and their better counterparts, insisting on the exemplary importance of good women for society at large: "aquí no se toca ni se pone mácula en las mujeres buenas y honradas, de las cuales hay muchas en cada ciudad, villa y lugar, que son honra de mujeres, espejo de honestidad y ejemplo de toda virtud" (Here we do not touch nor stain the good and honourable women, of which there are many in each city, town and place. They are the honour of women, a mirror of honesty and an example of all virtue) (San Jerónimo 69).

Madre Magdalena begins her proposal with an emphasis on the importance and necessity of the *galera* as a rehabilitative space. Although the jail was designed for the broadest range of female criminals to date, one of the major populations of interest to the *galera* was women who falsely posed as beggars: "hay otras muchas que, estando sanas y buenas y con fuerza para trabajar o servir, dan en pedir limosnas ordinarias" (There are many others that, being hearty and healthy and having strength to work or serve, beg for alms) (San Jerónimo 72). Madre Magdalena is concerned with these women because they exploit relatively new charitable systems created to assist the poor and sickly and put unnecessary strain on an already taxed system of social relief. Moreover she describes how some of these women pretend to have young children to provoke even more pity. The problem with the figure of the false beggar is the difficulty in proving whether or not the woman is actually destitute and unable to secure work. In many ways similar to the societal preoccupation with honour and blood purity, women too are required to display yet another set of often intangible characteristics: their relative degrees of health and wealth.[29]

The second major population of the institution is the same one targeted by the magdalen house: prostitutes, the majority under sixteen years old. The language used to describe the young prostitutes is far from sympathetic. Instead the author starkly emphasizes their animalistic and sinful qualities:

no se sustentan de otra cosa, sino de mal vivir. Para esto, llegada la noche, salen como bestias fieras de sus cuevas y portales de casas, convidando a los miserables hombres que van descuidados y, hechas lazos de Satanás, caen y hacen caer en gravísimos pecados

who live off nothing but unsavoury deeds. To this end, once night has arrived, they leave their caves like fierce beasts on the hunt. They place themselves by those cantons, in streets and homes' entryways, inviting those miserable men who wander carelessly and, being these ladies themselves lassos of Satan, they fall and make others fall into the gravest of sins. (San Jerónimo 71)

Prostitutes are dangerous in Madre Magdalena's view because of their libidinous appetite and especially because they are poised to trap men, bringing disorder upon themselves as well as the rest of society.

Madre Magdalena's principal concern with the false beggar and the prostitute is the poor example they set and the risk they pose to otherwise decent women: "Y es, que con su mal ejemplo y escándalo son ocasión y estropeado a muchas mujeres honestas y honradas para caer en semejantes maldades, o, a lo menos, verse en gran tentación y peligro de caer" (And it is that, with their bad example and scandal, they are a cause and a stumbling block for many an honest and honourable woman to stumble into such evils, or, at least, to see themselves among great temptations and in danger of falling to them) (San Jerónimo 75). In line with the humanists of the period, the nun depicts women's bodies as malleable sites of exemplarity and seeks to exploit that potential. Both women and men are cast as participants and observers to the performance of women's bodies. Erroneous behaviour elicits swift punishment, both public and private, designed to contain and rehabilitate.

The physical complex of the *galera* can be roughly divided into five major spaces: a bedroom, a workroom, a space for prayer, a secret jail, and a small kitchen. Upon entrance to the *galera*, women are asked to trade in old clothing for simple work clothes, eat a meagre bread-based diet, and are instructed on the many torture and punishment devices to be used on them if they violate the terms of their residence. As Madre Magdalena describes, "En esta casa ha de haber gran vigilancia y recato ... para esto han de tener cien ojos, valor y gran pecho, porque, si no, no se alcanzará el fin que se pretende, que es desterrar de la república la ociosidad y maldad de estas mujeres" (In this house there will be great vigilance and modesty ... for this it will have one hundred eyes, valour, and seriousness, because, if it doesn't, it won't accomplish the ends it desires, which is to banish from the Republic the idleness and evilness of these women) (San Jerónimo 80). To most successfully implement the *galera*, her proposal repeatedly emphasizes the need for severity and steadfastness.

The tension between the spectacle of deviance and its containment is evident even in the architecture of the *galera*. On the one hand, it is a space of strict confinement: "Esta casa ha de ser fuerte y bien cerrada, de manera que no tenga ventana, ni mirador a ninguna parte, ni sea sojuzgada de otra casa ninguna" (This house must be strong and well shut, in that it will not have any window or balcony in any part, nor will it be subjugated by any other house (San Jerónimo 77); on the other hand, the existence and function of the *galera* is no secret to nearby residents, as it is clearly marked with a sign that advertises its purpose. As Madre Magdalena describes in her proposal, the *galera* prominently features:

> Un letrero de letras tan claras y grandes que pueda ser leído de todos, que diga: "Esta es la Galera que su Majestad del Rey nuestro Señor ha mandado hacer para castigo de las mujeres vagantes, ladronas, hechiceras y alcahuetas, donde serán castigadas conforme a su culpa y delito."

> A sign with clear and large letters will be displayed for all to read: "This is the *galera* that His Majesty our King and Lord has created to punish vagrant women, thieves, sorceresses, and go-betweens, where they will be punished according to their fault and crime." (San Jerónimo 77)

Her design acts both as an announcement for the *galera* and as strategic self-promotion.

As an attentive businesswoman, Madre Magdalena conspicuously projects the image of her design in an array of visible places. The precision of her description at once clarifies the purpose of the institution and inscribes her own design into the architecture and explicitly highlights the royal approval and implementation of her design. Women who have entered the jail more than one time are also branded with a sign that represents the institution on the right side of their backs, "para que así sea conocida y se sepa haber estado dos veces en ella" (so that it will be known that she has been there two times) (San Jerónimo 81), a common practice of branding as a way record keeping.[30] In his dictionary Covarrubias discusses branding in various definitions including *hierro* (branding iron), *marcar* (to mark), *and esclavo* (slave), commenting on the origins of the practice and its frequent association with slavery, where for example he explains that the owl was a common insignia for Athens (536). For his own contemporary society, Covarrubias defines branding irons to be used to designate "pecado, delito o horror, error" (sin, crime or horror, error) (687). Although tattooing was a relatively widespread practice across Europe for both men and women, branding is important here because women's bodies become imprinted signs that indicate both purpose and possession. Women were branded with the coat of arms of the city or town where the jail was located, which again visibly displays the administrative and political approval of the nun's project through the fusion of institutional and municipal goals.

In this way, Madre Magdalena effectively makes use of both definitions of the word *galera* (galley) in the design of the jail. Although the word is most frequently associated with disciplinary sea-going vessels, it can also be used to describe early modern printing practices, which further solidifies the link between printing on paper and branding the body. As Dauge-Roth explains, it is even likely that branding irons themselves "with their raised Roman characters, were created by such specialized type designers, or at least produced in the same metal shops as punches and type" (135). The fact that women's bodies are marked with a generic brand representing the galley is also significant considering that up until this moment men would have been the only ones sentenced to the galleys, though it was likely that both men and women could have been branded with the same sign. The corporeal brand can be read as an extension of the *galera*'s sign described above and demonstrates the far-reaching display of Madre Magdalena's ambition and strategy, literally and metaphorically impressing her design onto the bodies of the women she aims to correct. The brand is a mark of shame for the women as well as an instructive reminder to others who might notice the brand on women's bodies, as if advertisements for the *galera* circulate wherever past offenders wander. That women's bodies are permanently and visibly marked as a past offender complicates the idea of clear redemption since the brand could never be removed.

The role of punishment inside and out of the *galera* oscillated between clear public displays like those described above and more private ones. Within the house, for example, violations of routine or order were met with swift punishment in secret zones of the house. Still, the presence of punishment and torture was public knowledge as a fact of life within the jail. Only in extreme cases did punishment move from a more hidden to a public location to serve a heightened and dramatic exemplary function. For example, the proposal describes a scenario in which a woman is unfortunate enough to be thrown back into the jail a fourth time. In this case, she would be hung at the front door of the *galera*. In Madre Magdalena's words this level of punishment ensures that "las demás escarmienten" (others will be warned) (San Jerónimo 81). Public hanging displays the crimes of the offender and the seriousness of the *galera* as a critical piece of the larger community.

Although an extreme and likely unusual occurrence, the public display of the punishment clearly broadcasts the severity of the institution to all nearby residents. Since the *galera* was designed as an exemplary space, the idea was to inspire fear in women in order to lead them to virtue: "que esta Galera será escarmiento, para que muchas mujeres perdidas se recojan a buen vivir, por el miedo y horror que cobraran a esta pena y castigo, temiendo no ser castigadas con tanta afrenta y rigor" (That this *galera* should be a warning so that many lost women will return to a good life through the fear and horror of penalty and punishment, now afraid of punishment with affront and rigour) (San Jerónimo 89). The *galera* perfected its ability to reform women both inside and out of the jail simply through the threat of such extreme punishment. Whether or not women actually observed such cases became irrelevant.

In many ways the daily routine of the jail, marked by a strict regimen of work and prayer, was very similar to the magdalen house model, yet the severe discipline of the institution was unique to the *galera* and many of the corrective practices were modelled after existing practices for men. It is known, for example, that women in magdalen houses were commonly not permitted to share beds, talk, or gossip while in their sleeping quarters; in the case of the *galera,* these provisions were even more strictly enforced. Some women were even chained or shackled to their beds to prevent unnecessary commotion: "duerman algunas de la mas inquietas con alguna cadena o en el cepo ... porque no estarán pensando sino por donde irse" (some of the most restless slept in chains or in the wheel clamp ... so that they would not be thinking about where they should go) (San Jerónimo 86). Madre Magdalena believed that the unique harshness of the *galera* allowed for more successful reformation of women. Likewise, Madre Magdalena argued that Spain as a whole would benefit through the reduction of sinful behaviour.

Through the development of stringent work and devotional practices and stricter punishment when necessary, the *galera* aimed to restore women to the same noble ends as the magdalen house: religious or married life. Her proposal emphasizes the transformative capability of the *galera*: "para que sirvan a Dios y dejen su mal vivir y se confiesen bien" (so that they may serve God and abandon their evil ways and confess thoroughly) (San Jerónimo 92). To protect so-called better women and the larger health of society, the nun argued for the containment of unruly women: "las podridas y malas, que afrentan la honestidad y virtud de las buenas con su disolución y maldad" (the rotten and evil women, who assault the honesty and virtue of good women with their dissolution and evil) (69). Her distinction between lesser women and their better counterparts was not unusual; Madre Magdalena's writing reflects the severe ideological climate of her time period, which enforced elaborate classification systems for women for the sake of maintaining social order. Yet, the proposal is especially significant because it is a woman that advocates for harsher punitive measures for women. Throughout the proposal she exhibits a powerful investment in the protection of women through the novel directive to swiftly and harshly punish those who threaten them.

Unruly women are dangerous according to the author because of their potential to beguile men and ruin otherwise decent marriages, an institution the nun recognizes as central to the protection and wellness of women. With that context in mind, Madre Magdalena advises that the *galera* instruct women to "servir mejor" (better serve) (San Jerónimo 90), as a way to improve domestic relations when they are released from the jail. Similarly she argues that the *galera* will "mejorar el matrimonio" (improve marriage) (San Jerónimo 90), because women will be better instructed as wives and mothers, and mainly because men will have fewer opportunities to ruin their marriages through affairs with lesser women. Finally, she insists that through the creation of a more effective disciplinary system, other charitable social institutions will "mejor funcionamiento" (work better) (San Jerónimo 90), thus more able to dedicate themselves to the aid of their specific populations. Ultimately, although the extremity and harshness of punishment for women was unique to the *galera* system, it also reflected Madre Magdalena's passionate investment in the protection of women.

III *Recogimiento* as a Women's Practice

Two images of the converted prostitute Mary Magdalene were prominently featured in the church of La Casa de Santa María Magdalena de la Penitencia. A life-like sculpture of the saint by Don Andres de los Elgueros sat prominently on the main altar. Nearby, over the side entrance of the church, was an original painting commissioned by the house from Juan Carreno de Miranda (1614–85).[31] In this larger-than-life image, *La Magdalena penitente* (1647), the saint is visually represented practising *recogimiento* in the desert with the conventional attributes of penance and contemplation. Perched under a dark cave and gazing upward towards the sky, Mary Magdalene is surrounded by the conventional attributes of contemplation: the skull (humility and penitence), crucifix (redemption), and the book (wisdom). Despite the intensity of her sacred contemplation, the painting also calls attention to a profane sexuality. Her long, luxurious hair barely covers her naked breasts and the lower half of her body is wrapped in a rich blue and gold fabric that recalls the frivolities of her worldly life. In the visual theatre of the church, the magdalen house commissioned an image of conversion that displayed the many contradictions of *recogimiento* that itself employed: at once private and displayed, sacred and profane. The house worked to eradicate the profanity of women's uncontained sexuality even as its holy mission was predicated on its existence.

After the Council of Trent, one of the most cultivated images in religious iconography was of Mary Magdalene in the desert. Offered by theologians to artists as a model of repentance, the saint became an important image for the Catholic model of confession. Clergymen preached to prostitutes about the merits of conversion on her feast days. Magdalen houses were erected across southern Europe based on the model of her conversion. Madre Magdalena de San Jerónimo too celebrated the saint's story as her religious namesake. In the Carreno de Miranda painting, Mary Magdalen enacts the contradictions of *recogimiento* and testifies to the way rehabilitation is a gendered practice. Even those completely redeemed and transformed (*arrepentida*) are marked by the extra dimension of profanity linked to their sex.

This book brings to the forefront two of Madrid's most well-known custodial institutions for women through an examination of the practices of rehabilitation crafted by the Casa de Santa María Magdalena de la Penitencia and Madre Magdalena's *galera*.[32] The comparison between the two institutions provides a more complete understanding of their institutional history and daily practice. Moreover, it offers a model for understanding the larger topic of rehabilitation for women at the centre of a complex spiritual and sexual economy. Spain's economic problems are redressed as moral issues directed particularly at women.

Also, women are punished for moral infractions, not just criminal acts. These scenes of rehabilitation demonstrate the interwoven religious, penal, and judicial discourses that framed the construction of these spaces. Moreover study of these institutions makes evident the tensions between rehabilitative models and practices as well as the varied objectives of each institution.

Rehabilitation is predicated on the idea of transformation: from corruption to virtue and sickness to health. While today the concept is most commonly associated with clear institutional practices, such as a hospital or halfway house, in the early modern period the topic of rehabilitation – as displays of punishment, religiosity, and penitence – took a variety of forms in a surprising array of places. The period is one obsessed with theatricality: a magdalen house performed elaborate entrance rituals in front of a portrait of conversion, the Inquisition staged *autos* in public squares, and Spain's public theatres were consolidated and professionalized under the general supervisor of the hospitals.

The following chapters take the link between theatres and custodial institutions as a point of departure in order to explore how popular theatre used the standard structure of the three-act comedy to dramatize women's rehabilitation, staging – like the Casa de Santa María Magdalena de la Penitencia and Madre Magdalena's *galera* did – their own set of reform strategies for women. The study of popular enactments of women's rehabilitation are mediated by the limits of the *comedia* as a genre; in Margaret Greer's words, "Spain's professional theater is 'at best a trick mirror that both represents and distorts, showing as often the myths of a society's self image as its realities'" ("Tale of Three Cities" 394). This inclusion of theatrical representations of women's rehabilitation offers a more complete account of the topic that gives credit to comic, dramatic, and parodied representations that were popular with a diverse audience. Because these scenes take place on stage, enactments of rehabilitation are always tied to public performance. *Unruly Women* examines the way these public enactments offer nuanced portrayals of rehabilitation through the insinuation of action that takes place offstage or outside of the script. This combination of public and private enactments of rehabilitation negotiates normative expectations for women's behaviour.

The *galera* and the magdalen house worked to transform women into "productive" members of society. The theatre, too, projected images of women transformed, domesticated, or suffering because of their inability to change. The book provides a comparative model between literary and historical seventeenth-century rehabilitation systems through an examination of the cultural status of the Spanish *comedia* and its intersection with the rise of custodial institutions in Madrid. As significant sources for the study of early modern Spanish women, the scenes of rehabilitation enacted by custodial institutions and *comedias* make apparent the intricate interplay between identity, resistance, and control inherent in the inquisitorial context.

PART TWO

2
Stage Widow in Pedro Calderón de la Barca's *La dama duende*

Pedro Calderón de la Barca's *La dama duende* (The Phantom Lady) (1629) narrates the familiar tale of the deviant woman transformed and domesticated by marriage.[1] Just months after Madrid consolidated its control over public theatres, whereby companies paid an amount of their profits directly to the city, which in turn paid a fixed sum to the hospitals, the widowed protagonist of the canonical comedy enacted a favourite role on the early modern stage. Like many trickster heroines of the *comedia*, Ángela eschews the solitary practice ascribed to her by contemporary moralists and instead crafts dramatic scenes designed to woo the object of her desire. The play's cunning protagonist escapes the obsessive confines of her brothers' care only to receive their blessing at the end of the play when she leaves their home to remarry.

Questions about how to interpret this canonical taming of the shrew are of course not unique to this play; they are quite familiar to scholars of early modern theatre. Next to Shakespeare's Katharina, Calderón's Ángela is one of the most famous embodiments of the character type within Spain, and is often compared to her predecessor Finea, the comic heroine of Lope de Vega's *La dama boba* (Lady Nitwit) (1613). Still, Ángela's story is a more multifaceted one because the drama of her marriage is complicated by the fact that it is not her first. The presence of the young and defiant widow in a range of literary and non-literary texts speaks to the importance of the figure throughout the period. In his seminal description of one of the most well-known literary widows, Doña Endrina of *El libro de buen amor* (The Book of Good Love) (1330), Juan Ruiz emphasizes the seductive qualities of the young widow that make the character type such a popular one, in particular the combination of her youthful beauty and sexual experience. Later moralists respond cautiously to this popular depiction of widows. Juan Luis Vives, for example, advises widows in *La educacción de la mujer cristiana* (The Education of a Christian Woman) (1524) on how to most favourably conduct themselves in mourning, at home and in public, to best safeguard their reputation. Meanwhile, in opposition to the advice proffered by moralists, the wily widow takes centre stage in Lope de Vega's *El perro del hortelano* (The Dog in the Manger) (1613) and *La viuda valenciana* (The Widow from Valencia) (1620), just years before Ángela makes her appearance in *La dama duende*.[2]

The topic of a widow resisting marriage puts the play into one of the most controversial yet commonplace conversations in regard to the proper place of women, and it is, in fact, the play's treatment of space that makes it one of the most compelling representations of the places of women's rehabilitation. Calderón's comedy contrasts the jail-like domestic sphere of Ángela's home with Madrid's bustling city streets. The protagonist's shape-shifting qualities as the Phantom Lady allow her the freedom to navigate between these two vastly different worlds, passing in and out of her strictly guarded confinement, exchanging letters, and consorting with spies. Her brothers' obsessive enactment of *recogimiento* is pitted against the freedoms offered by the city's public theatres as well as the domestic theatre of Ángela's own design, a practice of self-rehabilitation. The popularity of *La dama duende* as one of many comedies that put widows on the stage might also reflect the growing population of widows across Spain. For example, Stephanie Fink De Backer cites the 1569 census figures, where widows headed approximately 19.3 per cent of Toledan households (1). The representation of widows in the *comedia* frequently emphasizes their non-normative relationship to the marriage structure and offers examples of ways in which women can or should be reintegrated into the dominant structure.

An enormous body of critical literature has dealt with this canonical play from a variety of interpretive approaches, but has generally agreed on reading Ángela as the congenial protagonist. Barbara Mujica, for example, views Ángela as oppressed by the patriarchy of her brothers ("Tragic Elements"); Arthur Holmberg sees her as a purely comic widow ("Variaciones"); and, Catherine Larson emphasizes the protagonist's subversion and reaffirmation of societal norms ("La dama"). Most critical work has read the play's major theme as a battle between patriarchy and the individual and emphasizes how the clever protagonist "tricks" her brothers into allowing a happy marriage of her own design.[3] Feminist critics have also suggested that Ángela's status as an indebted widow is a way to create a sympathetic character. Larson, for example, describes Ángela's "economic martyrdom" (*Language* 99).

Early in the play it is explained that Ángela's responsibility for her deceased husband's debts binds her to the financial support of her brothers. Because of her financial situation and newfound dependence on her brothers, Ángela is forced to lead a life of strict seclusion:[4]

> su esposo era
> administrador en puertos
> de mar de unas reales rentas
> y quedó debiendo al rey
> grande cantidad de hacienda,
> y ella a la corte se vino
> de secreto, donde intenta,
> escondida y retirada,
> componer mejor sus deudas
> ... su estado no le da
> ni permisión ni licencia
> de que nadie la visite.

> Her husband was the Collector of the Royal Ports and when he died he owed the king a great deal of money, that I know. So now Doña Ángela has come to court in secret to try to pay her debts, living in rigorous confinement here ... this situation means no visitors. (331–44)[5]

The relationship between widows and their finances was a major preoccupation for early modern Spaniards. As the number of women confronted by the economic issues of their deceased husbands continued to increase, social reform measures were put into place to address these concerns. As Margaret Greer explains, "According to the old *Fuero juzgo*, a woman who remarried or committed adultery within a year of her husband's death forfeited half her dowry" ("The Self" 95). In the year immediately following a husband's death, women were required to observe a one-year mourning period. Although the Nueva Recopilación of 1569 made it possible for widows to marry during this period without financial penalty, this contextual information helps situate the story of Ángela's severe confinement and dependence on her brothers.

Calderón stages the problem of widows' debt inheritance not only for the sake of creating a sympathetic character, but also because they were prominent subjects of concern to his audience.

The status of widows in early modern Spain is complex, as De Backer explains: "Widowhood constituted a juridically emancipated status, where widows obtained considerably more legal freedom than married women ... The development of widows' strong position under law can be attributed to the demands of a frontier society, where unencumbered legal personhood fit the demands of communities often left without men in charge" (10).[6] The way that Ángela's brothers exert *recogimiento* as a rehabilitative practice onto their sister is somewhat difficult to explain. It may have to do simply with the fact that her family is preoccupied with protecting her dowry from creditors.[7] It is true that early modern widows assumed more significant legal responsibility; Thomas Kuehn writes, "Widowhood has also been described as a time of diminishing resources and growing poverty" (108).[8] For example, peasant women in Galicia suffered an economic decline after the death of their husbands; Allyson M. Poska explains, "According to Castilian law, only their marital property could be used to repay her husband's debts, not her dowry or any other property she had acquired" (173). Given that Ángela's marriage at the end of the play is depicted as freedom from her domestic jail, it is also worth speculating on how remarriage is depicted as a fiscally promising way out of debt for her as well as her family. *Recogimiento* as rehabilitative practice transforms Ángela from indebted widow to solvent wife.

While the "lusty" widow is a common figure of early modern literature, as Merry E. Wiesner-Hanks explains, "Studies indicate that women who could afford to resisted all pressure to remarry and so retained their independence" (95). Of course in Ángela's case, she does not yet possess the financial independence required to maintain her autonomy. Given her youthfulness and economic situation, Ángela receives the following cautious advice from her maid Isabel:

> Señora, no tiene duda
> de que mirándote viuda,
> tan moza, bizarra y bella,
> tus hermanos cuidadosos
> te celen; porque este estado
> es el más ocasionado
> a delitos amorosos;

y más en la corte hoy,
donde se han dado de usar
unas viuditas de azahar,
que al cielo mil gracias doy
cuando en las calle veo
tan honestas, tan fruncidas,
tan beatas y aturdidas;
y en quedándose en manteo,
es el mirarlas contento;
pues sin toca y devoción,
saltan más a cualquier son,
que una pelota de viento.

But dear madam, in light of your youth, your charms and sprightly ways, it's not surprising that your brothers take measures to protect you. There's nothing like a winsome widow to rouse crimes of passion, especially in Madrid where perfumed widows have grown so common. I thank the heavens a thousand times when I see them in the streets, so devout, so disapproving and demure, but when they cut loose, casting off both hoods and piety, how amused I am to see them bouncing about like balls upon any provocation. (ll. 402–20)

Isabel explicitly links Ángela with her youth, her wit, and her beauty. Though attractive qualities, they also prove dangerous because they can incite amorous crimes. According to Isabel, a widow's reputation is at risk because of the "viuditas de azahar," or the courtesans of the Spanish court, because they possess the sinister ability to transform between saintly and sexual figures. They also move transgressively from one lover to another as if they were a ball passed between players in sport. Ángela is thus circumscribed by the connections between widow, courtesan, and actress. All three figures are marked by the blessing and curse of their dramatic abilities and ambulatory lifestyles.

Throughout the play, Calderón emphasizes the severity of Ángela's forced seclusion. When, for example, Ángela first begs for Manuel's assistance in Madrid's streets, she describes herself as in the process of dying: "¡Adiós, adiós, que voy muerta!" (Good-bye, good-bye, I must hasten or die!) (112), clearly referring to the punishment awaiting her if she is caught outside of the confines of her home. Similarly, as Ángela flees, Cosme comically notes her instability: "!Es dama o es torbellino!"

(Was that a lady or a whirlwind?) (115). Parallel sentiments can be observed when the protagonist rushes to dress herself in her proscribed widow's attire when she first returns to her home:

> Vuélveme a dar, Isabel,
> esas tocas ¡pena esquiva!
> vuelve a amortajarme viva,
> que mi suerte cruel
> lo quiere así.

> Give me that widow's hood, Isabel; shroud me alive again, since that's what my cruel fate decrees. (369–73)

Seamlessly moving from the liberties of Madrid's public theatres to the confines of her home, Ángela likens her status as widow to a death sentence and shrouds her prominently youthful body in deathly garb.

Ángela's depiction of widowhood and the forced *recogimiento* she inhabits are also reflected in the proscriptive literature of the time. At the end of the sixteenth century, for example, Gaspar Astete examined the etymology of the word "viuda" (widow) when he wrote his treatise on the social condition. He writes, "vi, que es una partícula privativa, que quiere dezir fin, y dua, que quiere dezir dos y assi tanto es dezir viuda es sola sin la compañía de su marido" (*vi*, a single article which means "end" and *dua* which means "two," which therefore means the widow is alone without the company of her husband) (A2v). According to his reading, widowhood renders women to be fragmented or incomplete. Likewise, in Vives's treatise on widows' behaviour, he explains that she is constantly at risk: mourning too much or too little (299), or too eager or too reluctant to remarry (311). Like Ángela's brothers, Vives urges for the protection of widows: "A widow does not belong in the marketplace, in male gatherings, or in crowds. In those places, there is great danger for the virtues that are most honored in a widow – chastity, modesty, good reputation and holiness" (319).

In opposition to Vives's counsel, the opening scene of *La dama duende* depicts Ángela as she wanders the streets of Madrid, dressed provocatively in *corto tapada* (short veil), and visits the city's public playhouses and furtively engages in conversation with groups of men. As Laura Bass and Amanda Wunder have made clear, the early modern art of veiling functioned at once as a practice of concealment and seduction. Ángela's use of this suggestive garment in her first appearance on stage visibly marks the way she is interpreted by her audience.

The setting of the play – in Madrid – is also noteworthy. The dramatic growth of the city had profound impacts on its residents, particularly women. The dynamics of urban communities across Europe were in the process of change in the early modern period. As Laura Gowing argues, "Marriages ended earlier, because of higher mortality rates, and neighbours knew each other for shorter periods of time. The possibilities of urban anonymity raised fears about immorality, illegitimacy and prostitution. Larger numbers of single women, often mobile between households, could pose a threat to social, sexual and economic order" (*Common* 9). *La dama duende* comments specifically on the changing landscape of Madrid, when for example Manuel remarks that the new straight and narrow streets make it more difficult for Ángela to escape: "¡Oh qué derecha es la calle¡ / Aún no se pierden de vista" (They're still in sight, the street is so straight and long) (141–2). Nothing like the dark and winding streets of the medieval city, Madrid's new construction promotes clear and accessible paths with heightened attention to the visibility of its occupants and their transgressions.

In contrast to the modernized accessibility of Madrid's streets, the second space for women depicted in the play is in the strict domestic *recogimiento* enforced by Ángela's brothers. Although it was customary for widows to observe a one-year mourning period in seclusion, Ángela is zealously hidden away away in a secret compartment of her family house, a dark, ominous, and enclosed space that in many ways reflects the rigidity of the custodial institutions of the period. The extremity of her situation can be most clearly appreciated in Ángela's complaints, "¡Válgame el cielo! Que yo / entre dos paredes muera, / donde apenas el sol sabe / quien soy, pues la pena mía / en el término del día / ni se contiene ni cabe" (God be my witness, I'm dying within these walls where hardly a beam of sunlight can penetrate. By the end of the day I can barely support the misery of this prison) (379–84).

Ángela contrasts the limits of her confinement with the freedom she views in the theatre, metatheatrically signaling the allure of Spain's *corrales* to her audience:

Sin libertad he vivido,
porque enviudé de un marido
con dos hermanos casada;
¡y luego delito sea,
sin que toque en liviandad,
despuesta la autoridad,
ir tapada vea

un teatro en quien la fama
para su aplauso mortal,
con acentos de metal
a voces de bronce llama!
¡Suerte injusta, dura estrella!

What freedom is this, bereaved of a husband, to be wedded to a pair of brothers? And if I should defy their authority and in all innocence slip out under a veil to see the theatricals, open to all the city, where the bronze voice of fame rouses immortal applause, I would be considered a common criminal. How unjust and miserable is my fate. (390–402)

As a point of contrast to the stage, Ángela emphasizes the captivity of her home life, likening her living situation to the confines of a prison cell, and framing her relationship with her brothers as a second marriage.[9] The oppressiveness of Ángela's home is even emphasized in the details of its jail-like construction, with windows "con aldabas y rejas" (with locks and bars) (1038).

Angela's room is separated from the rest of the house by a door hidden behind an innovative piece of the set, a glass cabinet. At once fragile and sturdy, moveable and fixed, the meaning of this paradoxical contraption has received diverse interpretations from critics.[10] The cabinet is described in detail at the start of the first act:

Y más habiendo tenido
tal recato y advertencia,
que para su cuarto ha dado
por otra calle la puerta,
y la que salía a la casa,
por desmentir la sospecha,
de que el cuidado la había
cerrado, o porque pudiera
con facilidad abrirse
otra vez, fabricó en ella
una alacena de vidrios,
labrada de tal manera,
que parece que jamás
en tal parte ha habido puerta

Opening a doorway from the guestrooms out to another street, and block-
ing off the inner door leading to the rest of the house with a glass cup-
board so cleverly constructed that no one would imagine there had ever
been a door. (348–61)

Although the cabinet evidently serves as the key passageway to and
from Ángela's room, it is also marked by its transparency. The cabinet
puts Ángela on display while at the same time it contains her, again
echoing the position of the early modern actress both glorified and con-
strained by the limits of the stage. Luis points out the instability of the
cabinet when he complains, "pues ya dices / que no ha puesto por
defensa / de su honor más que unos vidrios, / que al primer golpe se
quiebran" (by your description, a mere pane of glass defends my sister's honor, a pane that a single stroke could break to smithers) (365–8).
The delicate material of the cabinet only draws attention to the fragility
of women's honour itself.

While the *comedia* provides insight into the logic of a rehabilitative
practice from a family's perspective, it also serves as an imaginative
space in which to represent a woman's personal response to her own
confinement. Almost immediately following her initial escape to the
public theatre from the confines of her home, Ángela's participation in
the theatre begins to infiltrate further into the domestic sphere. She ex-
tends her activities beyond designated theatrical spaces, and transforms
her home into a virtual theatre, where she masterfully takes on the roles
of director and lead actress in a romantic affair with Don Manuel. In
direct opposition to the confinement administered by her two brothers, Ángela teams up with her maid, Isabel, to literally construct a new
space in which to perform. This female alliance in a domestic theatre
parallels specific, contemporary realities about widows who wished to
be actresses. Although legally they were unable to perform because all
actresses were required to be married, Brooks explains how married
women of a company "would assume responsibility for a widow" in
order to circumvent the laws, as was the case of Sevillian women Mariana Jacinta (1619) and Francisca López (1663) (239).

Although Ángela was previously unaware of the secret possibilities of the glass cabinet, Isabel helps her navigate the passageway with
greater freedom and creativity. Isabel does not only inform Ángela of
the mobility of the glass cabinet, "aunque de vidrios llena, / se puede
muy bien mover" (one that is full of glass but that can still be easily

opened again) (591–2); she goes so far as to suggest the space be re-built altogether, using two fake nails to ensure that the door cannot be opened from the other side, and therefore only the two women share the secret of how to access the space (609–15). Spurred by Isabel's advice, the two women literally rebuild and assert control over the central passageway of the house and create a new space in which to perform.

Ángela manipulates the tools of the theatre to recover her own agency. She contrasts her current lack of freedom with the open space of the public theatre and the lure of its crowded and jubilant audience. In a conscious transgression of her ascribed role, Ángela secretly escapes a life of confinement so that she is able to enjoy the freedom of the theatre, where tragedy is witnessed and mourned instead of concealed. In this way, Ángela's participation in the life of the theatre represents a cathartic escape from her daily existence and serves as a kind of rehabilitation of her own design.

Ángela's prowess as director and actress becomes most evident as she pursues an affair with her love interest, Manuel, who has been invited to stay as a guest of her brothers. With Isabel's assistance Ángela tears through all of Manuel's possessions, envying his collection of personal fashion accessories and chiefly his toiletries. The scene depicts the anxieties (real or imagined) that surround a widow's intimate relationship with masculine property, namely his material goods and finances. The two women rifle through his love letters, steal a woman's portrait, and leave behind an extra letter in his room (883–90). In this letter Ángela officially creates roles for herself and Manuel, casting him in the role of "El Caballero de la Dama Duende" (The Gentleman of the Phantom Lady). While initially her amorous pursuit is merely a distraction from the boredom of *recogimiento*, she is increasingly motivated by a jealous inquisitiveness:

> Dijérate que mostrarme
> agradecida y pasar
> mis penas y soledades,
> si ya no fuera más que esto,
> porque necia y ignorante
> he llegado a tener celos
> de ver que el retrato guarde
> de una dama, y aun estoy
> dispuesta a entrar y tomarle
> en la primera ocasión,

y no sé cómo declarar
que estoy ya determinada
a que me vea y me hable

Call it a gesture of gratitude to our guest, or something to do to while
away the long hours of solitude. Yet it's something more than that. What
began in idle curiosity has now roused my jealousy, for among his belong-
ings I found the portrait of a lady, which I'm tempted to get as soon as I
can. Then I must find a way to let him know how determined I am to meet
and talk to him in person. (1270–82)

Ángela's role as actress and director allows her to express the desire to
both be seen and be spoken with, once again juxtaposing the confinement of her life as widow with the possibilities offered by her domestic
theatre.

Ángela's power over language, as writer of both personal correspondence and theatrical scripts, is further displayed when she undertakes a spontaneous performance as the Phantom Lady. With repeated
references to her powerful and ghostly qualities, Ángela utilizes the
strength of her own speech as a way to free herself from the grip of
her captors. She assertively commands both space and distance from
Manuel: "Generoso don Manuel / Enríquez, a quien está / guardado
un inmenso bien, / no me toques, no me llegues" (A great treasure
lies in store for you, oh, noble Don Manuel Enríquez. But if you touch
me ...) (2090–3). Ángela's formidable performance renders both Manuel
and Cosme speechless. Manuel is dumbstruck by the beauty of the appa-
rition, "Imagen es / de la más rara beldad / que el soberano pincel / ha
obrado" (Never has God's hand drawn so heavenly a portrait) (2040–3),
while Cosme only manages to iterate a series of stunned questions:
"Téngase el duende a la luz. / Pues, ¿qué es de él? / ¿No estaba preso?, /
¿qué se hizo?, ¿dónde está?, / ¿qué es esto señor?" (Now let's have a
look at this ghost. Where is he? Didn't you have your hands on him, sir?
What happened?) (1611–14). In sharp contrast to Ángela's prowess with
language, the scene ends with Cosme's incoherence and confusion.[11]

Motivated by her debut performance as the Phantom Lady, Ángela
conspires with Beatriz to undertake more elaborate scenes in pursuit
of her romantic affair. Ángela again relies on the support of her female
allies in the face of her brothers' meddling. Don Luis, for example, con-
fronts Ángela and Beatriz directly about their partnership, "¿Qué es lo
que las dos tratan, / que de su mismo aliento se recatan?" (What can

the two of them be plotting and hiding under their breaths?) (1781–2). In a move reminiscent of the capture of Don Juan in the final act of Tirso de Molina's *El burlador de Sevilla*, Ángela and Beatriz orchestrate an elaborate kidnapping of Manuel, employing tricks of lighting, costume, and script to create her scene. Beatriz subsequently affirms Ángela's role as director, by asking her for guidance:: "¿Y qué ha de ser mi papel?" (What role should I assume?) (2289). Ángela responds without hesitation and confidently casts herself in the role of the Phantom Lady and Beatriz as maid: "Agora el de mi crïada, / luego el de ver, retirada, / lo que me pasa con él" (To begin with, play a maidservant, and afterward from your hiding place you can watch what happens between us) (2290–2).

Juan unknowingly interrupts Ángela's rehearsal to question why she is wearing an elegant dress rather than her traditional widow's garb. She improvises with confidence and simultaneously criticizes the conventions assigned to women's mourning practices: "De mis penas y tristezas / es causa el mirarme siempre / llena de luto, y vestirme, / por ver si hay con qué me alegre, / estas galas" (I wear nothing but mourning garb all day to accompany my grieving memories. I thought these cheerful clothes might lift my spirits) (2447–51). Ángela successfully convinces her brother of her innocence, but is still critiqued for her defiance. Juan uses the opportunity to openly criticize what he sees as women's frivolity:

No lo dudo;
que tristezas de mujeres
bien con galas se remedian,
bien con joyas convalecen,
si bien me parece que es
un cuidado impertinente

No doubt they will. Fancy gowns and lavish jewels have always been a cure for women's sorrows. But this remedy seems merely impertinent. (2452–6)

Ángela's response to his critique bears repetition as it emphasizes the distinctiveness of her situation, as a figure of both seclusion and display: "¿Qué importa que así me vista, / donde nadie llegue a verme?" (What does it matter how I dress when no one comes to see me?) (2457–8). Once again, Ángela openly challenges the social codes assigned to widows in mourning. She also manages to exploit her family's pre-conceived ideas about women's frivolity. When her other brother Luis enters the room and comments on the assortment of plates and sweets that she had arranged as part of her performance, Ángela invokes the same commonly held belief about women's frivolity as a means to pro-tect herself and Beatriz: "¿Para qué informarte quieres / de lo que, en estando a solas, / se entretienen las mujeres?" (Why would you want to know what women do to pass the time when they're all alone?) (2694–7). Craftily alternating her rhetorical position based on the de-mands of her situation, Ángela's facility with language empowers her with the theatrical force necessary to advance her own position.

Ángela readily alternates between transgressive and proper behav-iour throughout the play. When her brother asks about her where-abouts during the afternoon, for example, she replies: "En casa me he estado / entretenida en llorar" (Weeping here in my room) (527–8). Rather than confess the truth about her outing, she carefully associ-ates the prohibited act of entertainment with the proscribed act of cry-ing. This meticulous word play stands at the centre of Ángela's folly, both adhering to and critiquing the norms ascribed to her social and sexual status. Her talent with dramatic language can be most fully ap-preciated through close study of her final monologue, an impressive eighty-four-line statement on the transformative power of her experi-ence as a widow in love. Opening again with a series of assertive com-mands: "Escucha, atiende" (Then hear me out) (2908), Ángela directs the attention of her audience and opens the space necessary to be seen and heard. The monologue offers the protagonist the opportunity to explain the conflict she has experienced between her role as widow and her personal desires as a young woman. She describes this conflicted state in ghost-like terms, emphasizing her own fragility and lack of confidence:

mi casa dejo, y a la obscura calma
de la tiniebla fría,
pálida imagen de la dicha mía,
a caminar empiezo;
aquí yerro, aquí caigo, aquí tropiezo
y torpes mis sentidos

I left the house, seeking the peace of the cold dark night. I wandered with-out direction, stumbling, falling, my senses stupefied. (2923–9)

Drawing attention to the prison-like qualities of both her silk dress and her brothers' home, she continues to describe the oppressive qualities of her life: "prisión hallan de seda mis vestidos; / sola, triste y turbada, / llego de mi discurso mal guïada / al umbral de una esfera / que fue mi cárcel, cuando ser debiera / mi puerto o mi sagrado" (trapped in the silk prison of my gown. In my sad and lonely confusion, my feet carried me back to my former prison, no longer my refuge and sanctuary) (2930–5). The significance of the comparison between the confines of jail and the dress and space assigned to her as widow cannot be overemphasized, as it speaks directly to the gendered particularities of rehabilitation designed and implemented by Ángela's brothers. Reflective of the institutional norms of the period, strict modesty and confinement are valued over women's individual expression or desire.[12]

Ángela also recognizes how her capacity with written and spoken language has permitted her various opportunities to protect herself from harm. In a provocative aside, she wonders aloud: "¿Quién creerá que el callar me ha hecho daño, / siendo mujer?" (Who would have thought a woman's silence could be the cause of ill when, in fact, a woman's silence can destroy her?) (2944–5). Despite the fact that reticence is frequently the preferred quality assigned to women during the period, in this monologue Ángela explains how her momentary hesitation to speak actually represents her downfall. Ángela loses her self-designed rehabilitative space and returns to the confines of her brothers' care. In turn, Ángela begins to represent herself in increasingly traditional terms, and emphasizes the volatility of her feminine constitution (physical, mental, and moral) in terms of the four humours: heat, cold, aridity, and moisture. Ángela describes herself as "hecha volcán de nieve, alpe de fuego" (like Etna frozen or a glacier on fire) (2950); her reliance on these conventional descriptions appears to intentionally undercut her own agency. She places responsibility on the socially constructed mechanics of her body (unstable, volatile) rather than her own volition as a way to free herself from blame.

Ángela is accused of being a "hermana fiera" (wicked sister) (2989) who has stained the family honour. Her life of confinement is explicitly framed as a punishment and cure for her offences: "dejarete encerrada donde segura estés, y retirada, / hasta que cuerdo y sabio / de la ocasión me informe de mi agravio" (I was to stay locked away and invisible while he found a way to redress this wrong) (2981–3). In response to one of the most direct insults of the play, Ángela's tone changes dramatically. In contrast to earlier scenes where she uses her words to acquire freedom, Ángela assumes a new speech of defectiveness to characterize herself as wholly dependent on Don Manuel:

> Mi intento fue el quererte,
> mi fin amarte, mi temor perderte,
> mi miedo asegurarte,
> mi vida obedecerte, mi alma amarte,
> mi deseo servirte
> y mi llanto, en efeto, persuadirte
> que mi daño repares,
> que me valgas, me ayudes y me ampares

> For love I sought your favor, and my only fear was losing you. My desire was simply to be cherished by you, to obey you from this day forth, to seal the bond between our souls and serve you. But now I must ask your aid in this moment of need – that you will shield, help and protect me. (2995–3002)

All of her actions link her explicitly to the second person status in which personal autonomy is erased in favour of a position of servitude. Likewise, the lack of conjugated verbs in this sentence speaks to Ángela's diminishing agency. The monologue concludes with a final series of requests, in which Ángela describes herself as imperfect and in need of correction from Manuel.

Despite the elaborate *recogimiento* established by her brothers, Ángela's path to redemption is relatively simple. In a matter of twenty-three lines, Manuel arranges a contract with Luis to marry Ángela:

> Esa mujer es mi hermana:
> no la ha de llevar ninguno
> a mis ojos, de su casa,
> sin ser su marido; así,
> si os empeñáis a llevarla,
> con la mano podrá ser

> Know, sir, that this lady is my sister and no man who is not her husband will, in my presence, carry her from this house. If you insist on leading her forth, you must immediately pledge to marry her. (3072–7)

In the classic exchange offer, Manuel quickly agrees to the terms of the arrangement. Ángela's otherwise dominant voice is completely absent from this process; in fact, she does not speak at all for the remainder of the play. Although Ángela's debt motivated the severe rehabilitative practices that dominate the bulk of the play, the issue of her debt is not explicitly raised at the play's end. Apparently because Ángela's brothers enthusiastically agree to the marriage arrangement, the entire family is cleared of the financial concerns that previously motivated the drama.

La dama duende's abrupt conclusion is not a surprise to scholars of early modern theatre. True to the formula of the *comedia*, Ángela relinquishes her power over language and theatre in exchange for the title of wife. Still the suddenness of the conclusion is more than merely conventional. Swift marriage is juxtaposed dramatically against the meticulous confines of domestic *recogimiento*. This sentiment is foreshadowed even in the first act of the play when Cosme utilizes the sword fight to poke fun at social convention that surrounds the fortification of widows. He compares the sword to a virgin who needs protection: "Es doncella; / y sin cédula o palabra, / no puedo sacarla" (Ah no, mine's a virgin, so she's not allowed out without a contract of marriage) (177–9). The commentary explicitly ridicules the details severity of Ángela's confinement.

La dama duende can be divided into three major sections: the contrast between the theatre and jail-like home administered by men, the interior theatre run by women, and the jail-breaking marriage negotiated by men. These distinct representations offer early modern scholars a range of opportunities to study the places and practices of rehabilitation for women, particularly those who occupy non-normative relationships to dominant social structures. In this case, the play is one of many *comedias* that focus on the status of widows and their relationship to marriage, a topic of great social concern in sixteenth- and seventeenth-century Spain. One of the most significant contributions of the play is its ability to expose the hypocrisy of both the logic and place of rehabilitation as well as its depiction of an alternate space of self-rehabilitation where women use theatre to cure what ails them.

One final scene illustrates this point: though Luis is the most fervent advocate for his sister's containment, early in the play he is presented as a character who is easily enticed by the charms of other women. When he spots a mysterious lady (his sister) entertaining a group of men on the street, he is unable to obtain her attention and later complains about his troubles to his sister. Ángela's response is a self-reflexive account on the "problem" of unruly women:

¡Miren la mala mujer
en que ocasión te había puesto!
¡Que hay mujeres tramoyeras! /... /
Por eso estoy harta yo
de decir, si bien te acuerdas
que mires que no te pierdas
por mujercillas, que no
saben más que aventurar
los hombres

Upon my word, are there still such sirens who lead men into snares? Such
heartless scheming women? ... You'll remember how I've warned you
not to fall for women who only lead men into compromising adventures.
(515–25)

Ángela's response espouses her brothers' containment logic and re-
flexively celebrates her own transgressions. By comparing herself to
the novelty of a theatre's *tramoyera* (trapdoor), she marks her ability to defy expectation and provocatively inscribes her physical self
with the materiality of this theatrical innovation. Self-identification as
a "bad woman" is a self-deprecating joke directed to her brother as
well as, and perhaps more important, a self-congratulatory aside to
the audience.

Widows are a popular character in literature because they are seductive, scheming, and often comic. In the *comedia* especially, the formulaic
plot and structure offers to its audience a pleasurable and seemingly
innocuous encounter with a character that in real life incited serious
social concern. Ángela's comic description of the "bad woman" allows
audiences through laughter to consider the severity of expectations directed towards women and to the social practices that defined their everyday life. Though the nation sought to control and project a carefully
calculated image of circumspect behaviour for women – and widows
in particular – public theatre provided the space to imagine and even
celebrate alternatives. Likewise through the play's depiction of a variety of places and modes of rehabilitation, audiences can consider how
these divergent models confirm or contradict their own expectations.
Though Calderón only imagines a woman's voice of protest, the following chapter allows us to examine how a female author takes on a parallel topic, and explores new places and modes of women's rehabilitation
as enacted by women themselves.

3

Dramatizing Women's Community in María de Zayas's *La traición en la amistad*

At the onset of María de Zayas's *comedia, La traición en la amistad* (The Betrayal of Friendship) (1630), the protagonist of the play, Fenisa, commits the ultimate betrayal when she finds herself taken with her best friend Marcia's love interest. Although she is conflicted about her obligations to Marcia, Fenisa is ultimately willing to sacrifice their friendship for the sake of her personal desire. Fenisa does not merely pursue this new affair with Liseo, but, true to her assertive character, she does so flagrantly and worse yet, in tandem with other romances, repeatedly rebuffing the criticism she receives from betrayed friends and lovers.

Perhaps inspired by the vixen in Lope de Vega's comedy *El anzuelo de Fenisa* (Fenisa's Hook) (1617), María de Zayas y Sotomayor's (1590–?) depiction of her own Fenisa complicates the more familiar representation of the picaresque prostitute popularized onstage in Lope's comedy and inspired by her literary parents *La Lozana andaluza* (The Lusty Andalusian Woman) (1528) and *La Celestina* (Celestina) (1499). But Zayas's Fenisa is not a prostitute. Rather, she is an elite, single woman characterized for her promiscuity and her non-normative relationship to the rules of sex and gender. *La traición* is unique because it is one of the only representations of this character type from the perspective of a woman. Zayas was one of five known female dramatists in Spain who wrote *comedias* for performance, and like other playwrights of her generation she was well attuned to the usefulness of displays of penitence and punishment for the purpose of exemplarity.[1]

The most significant contribution of Zayas's representation of Fenisa as vixen is the extent to which her presence dramatizes the policing function of female friendship in the *comedia*. Lisa Vollendorf has repeatedly signalled the dearth of critical literature on the topic of friendship between women in early modern Spain and has helpfully highlighted *La traición en la amistad* as a site "in which the audience glimpses the workings of women's friendships [where] the importance of women's cooperation takes center stage" (*Lives* 273). *La traición* offers a unique representation of female friendship gone wrong, depicting the expectations of these social relations as well as critiquing their limits. The play portrays a complex and sometimes contradictory social scene, where women are obligated to police and protect the norms of their community even to the detriment of one another. Fenisa's devious presence would have likely been popular with her audience because of the comic appeal of her outrageous behaviour and also because her actions illuminate contemporary concerns about the regulation and construction of a female community and its norms.[2] By situating the play's representation of this community within prominent historical examples, it is possible to contextualize and interpret the weighty significance of this deviant heroine.

Like the majority of playwrights of her time, Zayas was influenced by Lope de Vega's *Arte Nuevo de hacer comedias* (1609), which required new works of theatre to both instruct and entertain. The task of uncovering the exemplarity of Zayas's heroine is difficult for a number of reasons, mainly because we have limited knowledge about the staging and performance of *La traición en la amistad*.[3] It is also uncertain whether the play was meant for popular consumption or was designed for a more exclusive (perhaps all-female) audience.[4] Whether Fenisa should be celebrated for her (arguably masculine) amorous prowess or criticized for the threat she poses to her peers is a question that continues to divide current scholarship on Zayas's only extant play.[5] Gwyn Campbell, Catherine Larson, Matthew Stroud, and others have pointed to Fenisa as a feminized Don Juan and emphasized her role as a negative example, while Laura Gorfkle, Valerie Hegstrom, and Constance Wilkins have focused on how the play depicts a positive model of the female community targeted against a common enemy, Fenisa.[6] On the one hand, to condemn Fenisa as the villain of the play celebrates the policing function of the female community, where women are bound together through the virtue of protecting cherished social and sexual norms. On the other hand, reading Fenisa as a feminized Don Juan emphasizes her excessive and socially disruptive qualities.

Although these two critical approaches to *La traición en la amistad* offer different interpretations of the play, what I want to highlight here is the way in which they also overlap. In both cases, Fenisa is marked for her "bad" behaviour; to borrow Campbell's words, Fenisa "is the 'bad' example" (484). Even when Fenisa is read as the heroine of the play, critics often justify her misdeeds through emphasis on the constraints of her social circumstances. While this may allow Fenisa the space to have several lovers, she is still admonished for deceiving her female friends. Although it is logical that the "betrayer" of friendship should suffer the unkind punishment of exclusion from marriage while the rest of her friends couple off and marry, this chapter examines the implications of such a classification in the context of her relationship to the norms of female sociability. Though scholars tend to idealize relations between early modern women, Laura Gowing provocatively claims, "If we are to understand the flexibility and heterogeneity that kept early modern patriarchy powerful, it becomes imperative to take seriously the parts women played in maintaining it as well as resisting it" (*Common Bodies* 6). Taking her assertion as a point of departure, this chapter argues that the figure of this unruly vixen plays a significant role in informing the construction of female community, both within the confines of the play and within the broader setting of early modern Spain.

The critical celebration of the female community depicted in this play is easy to appreciate when we consider the obstacles women had to overcome to befriend one another in early modern Spain. For example, Vives argues that women are not to confide in each other even under dire circumstances. In the event a husband punished his wife physically, she was to remain silent in order to respect the integrity of her familial hierarchy:

> Devora tu dolor en tu casa y no lo cacarees fuera ni con otras te quejes de tu marido, que no parezca que pones un juez entre él y tú: encierra los sinsabores domésticos en las paredes de tu casa; ni salgan a la calle, ni cundan por la villa. Así, con tu comedimiento, harás más comedido a tu esposo, a quien, por otra parte, con tus quejas y futilidad ofensiva de tu lengua agravias más y más.

> Devour your grief at home; do not broadcast it in the neighbourhood or complain to others about your husband so that it may not appear that you appoint a judge between him and you. Keep domestic problems within the walls and threshold of the house so they will not be spread abroad. In this way you will render your husband more amenable when you would only further exacerbate him with your complaints and your useless tongue. (1094)

Although *La traición* focuses on single women, Vives's advice to young wives presses on the issue of patriarchal authority in the family. The example of Vives's instruction dramatizes what is most unusual about Zayas's play, where female friends freely interact with one another and use their networks with the purpose of protecting their own reputations. Principally important in this context is the way Laura directly petitions Marcia for guidance to recover her lost honour and how the absence of Marcia's father makes possible the drama of the story, where women are allowed to collaborate without male supervision. In Vives's view this kind of collaboration was indicative of an unstable patriarchy and allowed women protections and resources he felt they did not deserve.[7]

Despite the pervasive influence of humanist thought in early modern Europe and its affinity for female isolation and containment, recent scholarship has also shown that women were able to form networks, both political and social.[8] While these collaborations could take on subversive forms, as Zayas's play demonstrates, they also could take on a policing function, where normative behaviour is enforced for the sake of protecting the female community. In early modern Spain, Laura Gorfkle explains, "The female community was an entity of social control that worked to bring young women's conduct into alignment with social and moral norms" (615). This point is persuasively illustrated through a concrete historical example. Magdalena de Guzmán, the Marchioness of Valle, stands out as an intensely fascinating case of the power and perceived threat of female networks.

Magdalena de Guzmán was one of Margarita of Austria's ladies-in-waiting until 1601, and later became the governess of the infant, Ana, and finally the queen's *Camarera mayor de Palacio* (First Lady of the Bedchamber) as well as the Duke of Lerma's most immediate spy over the queen. Although as Magdalena Sánchez explains, her position was initially designed in a way that would allow Lerma to have control over the queen's activities, Magdalena de Guzmán instead "won the queen's favor ... and actually began to constitute a political threat" (*The Empress* 101). In response, she was tried for abuse of office, imprisoned, and exiled from the court in 1603.

What is most intriguing about this case is the severity with which Lerma responds to the threat of the female community. Sánchez describes how, during her trial, the duke sought to arrest de Guzmán's network of female friends, which included the Marchioness of Castellar (*The Empress* 101). The friendship between the two women was most closely scrutinized through an attack on the written correspondence they exchanged: "mandan que se miran a todos sus papeles y cartas y entre ellas hallaron por gran desgracia una carta q(ue) la Marquesa del Castellar a su grande amiga la avía escrito consolándola" (he ordered that they look at all of the papers and letters, and among them there was, unfortunately, a letter that the Marchioness of Castellar had written in order to console her).[9] Women strategically used means deemed appropriate to their sex, in this case letter-writing, and subverted them with the intention of promoting their own cause.

The threat of female communities working the "wrong" way led to revision of the *etiquetas* (protocol) of the queen's household in which Lerma worked to find ways to limit the queen's contact with the outside world and, as Sánchez notes, specifically with other women (*The Empress* 103). The case underscores the instrumental role that women often had in maintaining social norms (Magdalena's initial role as spy for Lerma), and the punishment of isolation and exclusion ascribed to women who subverted this precarious structure (Magdalena's exile from court). There are even examples of actresses who sustained patriarchal norms through their relationships to other women. Mary Blythe Daniels, for example, explains how many of the wealthiest actresses had female slaves "which traveled with them and sometime performed. The actresses also participated in dances and *entremeses* which belittled Africans and Indians" (169). Reading Zayas's play in the context of these cases draws attention to the obligations and constraints placed on powerful elite women. It likewise exposes the policing power of female communities and the hypocrisy of some of its norms.

In *La traición en la amistad*, the female community is initiated and defended primarily by women and the deviant female subject pays the price of exclusion at the end of the play.[10] In its simplest form, Zayas's play offers an evocative example of the contrast between women who play by the rules and one who breaks them. The plot revolves around several love triangles, and is initiated appropriately, with the betrayal of friendship. When Sebastián de Covarrubias defines the word *traición* (betrayal) – a key term that appears multiple times throughout the play – in his 1611 *Tesoro de la lengua castellana o española*, he provocatively argues that those who commit the crime of betrayal should be punished with blindness: "El pago que le dieron fue sacarle los ojos, con que vivió el resto de su vida miserable y abatido" (The punishment they gave him was to take out his eyes, so that he would live the rest of his life miserable and fallen) (914). This definition highlights the exemplary role of punishment, both in terms of physical discipline and containment. While those who follow the rules are allowed to "see," that is to say, they are granted particular social liberties, those who break the rules are literally "blinded," or physically contained, "placed in the dark."

The practice of containment took a variety of forms for women, as a family-run *recogimiento*, as depicted in *La dama duende*, or in a variety of other institutional forms, like the magdalen house or *galera*. Since Fenisa has broken the social code by virtue of her "bad" behaviour, the play's ambiguous punishment is suggestive. Instead Zayas brings to the forefront of her play the category of "betrayal" as a new type of crime for women. Fenisa enacts various kinds of betrayal (choosing love over friendship, having multiple lovers, celebrating her own promiscuity) and her community defines her transgressions in numerous ways (disloyalty, lack of discretion, dishonourableness, etc.).

Although love intrigues were a common theme of the baroque theatre, this play stands out for its focus on a female instigator of multiple affairs. Fenisa says of herself:

Hombres, así vuestros engaños vengo
… Mal haya la que solo un hombre quiere,
que tener uno solo es cobardía;
naturaleza es vana y es Hermosa

Men, this is how I get even with you and your tricks … Cursed be the woman who loves only one man, because it is cowardly to limit yourself to a single lover. (Zayas 1467–78)[11]

Radically departing from the idealized image of women proposed by the Renaissance humanist tradition, Fenisa acts according to her own free will, and aggressively pursues a number of men, encouraging others to follow her example, ignoring the wishes of her female friends, and using deception "the wrong way" by prioritizing personal desire without respect to women's community. In doing so, she exposes a double standard, not only between men and women, but also among women.

The hypocrisy of the community becomes evident when women are allowed to disrupt social norms in the name of protecting friendship and community, but are condemned to containment when their actions threaten this community. This is made explicit in Marcia's desire to punish Fenisa's betrayal, "¡Mal haya quien en tal tiempo / tiene amigas!" (The woman who has female friends these days has plenty of heartache!) (1082–3). Marcia directly suggests that Fenisa's violation of the codes of friendship will lead to her downfall.

If we read Marcia as the "good" friend, a community leader defending the rights of women, *La traición* makes explicit the conflict between "good" and "bad" women, examines how containment and circulation relate to the development of social norms, and, moreover, examines the implications of deviations from the norm by focusing on a protagonist, Fenisa, who refuses discretion. As she claims later in the play, instead of loving one person selfishly and exclusively, she offers her love to anyone who will accept it. As a vixen, she embodies excess and promiscuity: "Tengo la condición del mismo cielo, / que como él tiene asiento para todos / a todos doy lugar dentro en mi pecho" (I have the same disease that heaven has, because since God has room for everyone near him, I can make room for all those men instead in my heart) (2396–8). As Lucrecia appropriately responds: "También en el infierno hay muchas sillas / y las ocupan más que no en el cielo" (There is also plenty of room in hell, and it is fuller than heaven) (2399–400), she emphasizes the moral constraint central to the play's action. This interchange between the two women is especially noteworthy considering the heavy regulations placed on women's behaviour. Since Fenisa is unwilling to play by the rules ascribed to her sex, she is outcast from her community.

Throughout the play, women are categorized within a variety of descriptive binaries. In the first act, for example, when Liseo attempts to decide between his multiple love interests, he weighs his opinions of the three protagonists: Laura, Marcia, and Fenisa. In doing so, he attempts to categorize them according to their degree of "womanliness." For Liseo, Laura is "no es mujer" (not a woman) (1281) since she has already lost her virginity to him. In contrast, Marcia "es un ángel" (is an angel) (1282) because she is still a virgin, and is therefore socially accepted and alluring. However, Liseo is unable to categorize Fenisa. She is simultaneously "una diosa" (a goddess) (1282) but has surrendered "a mi afición" (to my affection) (1285). Both goddess and whore, Fenisa treads a social line that complicates Liseo's strict categorization of women. This inability to read Fenisa ultimately leads him to choose Marcia for his wife. He says, "Marcia en eso será la preferida" (Marcia would be the one I would choose) (1289). Personal desire does not play a role in his selection; rather Liseo's decision reflects the social norms concerning the expectations of marriage, in which the husband dominates a submissive and virginal wife-to-be.[12]

In order to demonstrate the policing nature of female friendship, it is useful to explore textual examples of the social manipulation that is allowed in the name of preserving friendship. Specifically, this chapter focuses on acts of deception committed to save Laura's honour. As mentioned earlier, Laura was the ex-lover of Liseo, but is abandoned by him when he falls in love with Marcia. In act 2 Laura puts her reputation on the line when she openly admits her dishonour so as to collaborate with Marcia. Laura travels independently to Marcia's home, conceals herself in a large cloak, and after a successful conversation with Marcia, crafts a letter to Liseo in which she falsely claims she has entered a convent. Laura justifies her deceit in the following way, "yo sé que su poco amor / dará lugar a mi enredo" (Knowing how little love he has for me, that will open the way for me to work my mischief) (1063–4). The two women collaborate to recover her reputation and lost honour.

Marcia not only affirms Laura's "transgressive" behaviour, but also assists her in composing the letter. In doing so, she solidifies their alliance:

> sabiendo
> que te tiene obligación,
> desde aquí de amarle dejo.
> En mi vida le veré.
> ¿Eso temes? Ten por cierto
> que soy mujer principal
> y que aqueste engaño siento

> now that I know he has a prior commitment to you, from this moment on I vow to stop loving him. I will never see him again as long as I live. Were you afraid of how I would react? Well know this: I am a noble woman, and I am so sorry about the way he deceived you. (1000–6)

Marcia's affirmation underscores the importance of her actions in relation to her social status; as a leading lady her actions are exemplary. She must assist Laura in avenging her dishonour not only for her own sake but also out of her obligation and commitment to her community of women. For these reasons, this scene makes clear that women are allowed to manipulate convention only when working to restore set norms.[13]

Another example of women's free circulation and deception appears in act 3, when Marcia and Laura create a literal performance for Liseo in an effort to restore his commitment to marry Laura. In an elaborate scene, the two women converse with Liseo from Marcia's window, only Marcia pretends to be Belisa (her cousin) while Laura pretends to be Marcia. Laura struggles with her performance and explains to Marcia: "Estoy tan triste que hablar / no puedo" (I am so sad I cannot even speak) (1995–6). Marcia has no sympathy for Laura's complaint, but instead emphasizes that her performance is crucial to the success of their scheme: "Mucho desdices / de quien eres. ¿Qué es aquesto?" (You are not showing what you are made of. What is this?) (1997–8). Laura's difficulty in the performance is understandable because she is asked to "be herself" by playing the part of Marcia. At the same time, Marcia's commitment to her part puts on display her fervent desire to restore Laura's honour, again privileging the women's community over private concerns. The women's subtle manipulation of Liseo's courtship satisfies their taste for vengeance and restores harmony to the social scene.

Even though Laura realizes this performance is necessary, she is more hesitant and thus less exemplary of a model. For example, later in the scene she becomes disgusted with Liseo's affection for Marcia (whom Laura pretends to be). Unable to contain her anger, she swiftly exits from the balcony scene. Her early departure leaves Marcia (as Belisa) to negotiate with Liseo, and again the scene displays Marcia's ardent commitment. When Liseo asks how he can repair his relationship with his lover, Marcia takes the opportunity to suggest a contract, in which he would promise marriage. She explains to Liseo that the contract is necessary because it will help to appease jealousy. She states: "Una mujer celosa / es peor que la víbora pisada" (A jealous woman is worse than a viper that has been stepped on and provoked) (2070–1), self-consciously signalling her own dangerous qualities, although she never allows her emotions to negatively impact her behaviour.

Calm and collected, Marcia deftly negotiates with Liseo. After the contract is sealed, Belisa justifies their actions in a monologue:

Laura será tu muger;
a quien [es] tu fe deudora,
que si engañando has vivido

y de ti engañada ha sido,
hoy tu engaño pagarás,
y por engaño serás,
a tu pesar, su marido.

Laura will be your wife, since you owe your faith to her. Because you have
lived by trickery, and she has been tricked by you, today you will pay for
that deceit, and you will be tricked into becoming her husband, whether
you like it or not. (2270–6)

In this sense, and according to the honour- and order-focused men-
tality of the time, Laura, Marcia, and Belisa are permitted to freely circulate and manipulate social convention because they are working to
restore the women's community and to isolate those who disrupt it,
namely Fenisa. Belisa's insistence here on the role of *engaño* is suggestive, as it reflects the capaciousness of the term. On the one hand, she
condemns Liseo for his deceptive *engaño*; as Covarrubias's definition
of the word explains, this would include "lo falso, engañador, el burlador" (false, swindler, trickster) (238). At the same time, she celebrates
the craftiness of their plan against Liseo as a successful form of *engaño*.
In Covarrubias's words: "el que engaña muestra voluntad, y gana de
una cosa, y haze otra ... porque el engañado siempre queda perdido ...
el que engaña es ingenioso y astuto" (He who tricks shows will, and
as he wins one thing he makes another ... because he who is tricked
always loses ... the trickster is clever and cunning) (238). This definition
allows the women to take ownership over their *engaño* as a legitimate
tool worth wielding, particularly as it allows them to protect their own
community.

The male characters unite at the end of act 2 when they also decide
to punish Fenisa for her transgressions. Don Juan, who had courted
Fenisa prior to renewing his commitment to Belisa, has been invited
to meet Fenisa at the park and instead finds her finishing a romantic
picnic with Liseo. Once Liseo leaves, Juan approaches Fenisa about her
indiscretion. Fenisa shows no embarrassment about being caught with
another lover because she never claims to be faithful to any single one.
She sees no harm in maintaining multiple relationships, and no reason
to hide her affair from Juan. As she points out later in the play:

Si mi amor [daña a] un alma porque tiene
sufrimiento en sus penas y tormento,

yo, Amor, que amando a muchos, mucho siento;
no es razón que tu audiencia me condene;
razón más justa, Amor, será que pene
la que tiene tan corto pensamiento
que no caben en él amantes ciento

If my love wounds another soul, causing it to suffer storms and pains, I,
Love, who love many men, feel that suffering a hundred times over; that
is no reason to condemn me. It would be fairer Love, if the one who suffers
is the short-sighted woman who does not make room in her heart for those
hundred other men. (2367–71)

Fenisa repeatedly refuses to apologize for her indiscretion and instead
she seeks to portray her promiscuity as a noble form of generosity.

Don Juan's desire to punish Fenisa springs from the fact that her actions
make visible what should have been kept discreet. Unlike Marcia, Fenisa
does not respect the rules of social engagements. Although Juan initially
intends to seek a violent revenge, he chooses instead to band together
with the other men whom she has "deceived." Following Marcia's exemplary model where emotions are second to reason, he explains to Belisa,
"Dejé sangrientas venganzas, / y para mayor afrenta / con la mano de
su cara / saqué por fuerza vergüenza, / diciendo, 'Así se castigan / a las
mujeres que intentan / desatinos semejantes / y que a los hombres enre-
dan'" (I left aside bloody revenge, and for even greater insult, I slapped
her, saying "that is the punishment for women who use such tricks and
try to ensnare men") (1744–51). Although it appears that Juan's actions
are part of his renewed commitment to Belisa, he seems more gratified to
publicly and visibly punish Fenisa's transgression, and ensure that others follow his example by initiating the creation of a solidified male community (formed in its opposition to a woman who threatens it).

Belisa affirms Juan's actions later in the scene, claiming they are ad-
mirable because of his restored commitment to her, and because Fenisa
has been taught a lesson about her inability to be "discreet" and "lady-
like," and about the consequences of such misbehaviour. She explains:

ninguna muger,
si se tiene por discreta,
pone en opinión su honor,
siendo joya que se quiebra.
Pues si lo fuera Fenisa,

esos engaños no hiciera / ... /
siempre dije que no es buena
la fama con opinions

No woman, if she considers herself prudent, puts her honor up for public discussion, since it is a precious jewel, easily broken. If Fenisa were circumspect, she would not do what she does, putting her reputation on the line that way ... I have always said that it is not good to link your reputation to public opinion. (1764–74)

Belisa makes clear that any principled woman would know better than to violate the norms of her community. Although Belisa, Laura, and Marcia have also deviated from convention, it is always in the name of restoring the women's community. In contrast, Fenisa does not respect her social obligations, and it is her carelessness that merits criticism and punishment. As a vixen, Fenisa prioritizes her own desires over the needs and obligations of her female community.

In contrast, the other characters in the play always prize public opinion over private concerns. Laura and Marcia, for example, accept unfaithful (Liseo) or unloved (Gerardo) husbands for the sake of protecting their status as honourable women. As Liseo notes at the opening of act 1, since Laura was betrayed she could not be socially recognized as an honourable woman without him. And as Marcia comes to understand in act 3, she must take Gerardo as her husband for the sake of protecting the norms of the community. She explicitly illustrates her recognition of these responsibilities in the following lines:

Calla, necia,
que sólo por ser muger,
no te echo por la escalera.
¿Dudas, Liseo? ¿Qué es esto?
Pues para que ejemplo tengas,
mira como doy mi mano
a Gerardo, porque sea
premiada su voluntad

Hush, you idiot; the fact that you are a woman is all that is keeping me from throwing you down the stairs. You are still not sure, Liseo? Well just so you will have a good example to follow, see how I am giving my hand to Gerardo as a reward for his good will. (2844–51)

Although Marcia is angry with Fenisa, again she controls her emotions, adopting the appropriate behaviour for interacting with another woman. Marcia models appropriate, gender-specific behaviour as she chooses Gerardo as her husband and facilitates the marriage between Liseo and Laura. At the close of the play, both men and women are forced to identify the marginal, in the form of Fenisa, with the purpose of enforcing the norms of their community.

On the other hand, Fenisa's violation of social codes is never justified within the world of the play. Although she, like other characters, violates social convention for her own self-interest, Fenisa never attempts to conceal her actions. Instead, she openly celebrates her transgressive behaviour and describes her actions as a result of her infinite capacity for love: "Los quiero, los estimo, y los adoro / a los feos, hermosos, mozos, viejos, / ricos y pobres, sólo por ser hombres" (I love, esteem and adore the ugly and the handsome ones, young boys and old men, rich and poor, and only because they are male) (2393–5). According to Fenisa's formulation, her love is infinite and not exclusive. Fenisa rejects the conventions ascribed to her sex in order to pursue her own desires. The conflict between Fenisa's desire and the demands of the female community is evidenced from the opening of the play, when she falls in love with Liseo's portrait and hesitates momentarily: "El amor y la amistad / furiosos golpes se tiran. / Cayó la amistad en tierra / y amor victoria apellida" (Love and friendship are fighting it out; friendship is defeated and love emerges victorious) (171–4). Zayas makes clear that by choosing desire over friendship, Fenisa is excluded and punished.

When Fenisa is cast out from the marriage scene at the end of the play, León ironically remarks that he will act as go-between for Fenisa and any interested audience member: "Señores míos, Fenisa, / cual ven, sin amantes queda; / si alguno la quiere, avise / para que su casa sepa" (My lords, as you can see, Fenisa is left alone without a single lover. If one of you is interested, let me know and I will pass on her address) (2911–14). León mocks Fenisa's availability and in fact puts her on the market as if she were a prostitute. While the comment certainly makes light of Fenisa's character, his remark does not explicitly condemn her for it in the conventional ways. In fact, Fenisa's marginalization at the end of the play guarantees her an unusual amount of freedom. Rather than being sentenced to death or marriage as would be typical of a standard *comedia de enredos* (comedy of errors), Fenisa is instead banished from her own social group. Although Fenisa is silenced and excluded at the end of the final scene, I argue that Zayas takes advantage of the heroine's prominent presence throughout the rest of the play.

The vixen's devious presence and her actions make social norms and her conscious decision to betray them readily apparent. Her dealings and interactions with the other characters offer a variety of instances that illustrate the intricate workings of early modern female relations in Spain, specifically as networks that function to protect social status and guard gendered norms. Although the end of the play excludes Fenisa from the marriage plot, the play is about more than just Fenisa's punishment.

Here it is worthwhile to turn to the question that started this chapter: why are critics so attached to viewing Fenisa as a "bad" woman? Fenisa violates social norms, and the play offers a moral lesson about the importance of the female community. Yet when Fenisa is read as simply the antihero of a harmonious women's community, we fail to notice the ambiguities of her character and the way in which she also stands for alterity and difference. In her work, *Against the Romance of Community*, Miranda Joseph questions the unambiguously positive representation of community especially as it is linked to women and portrayed by feminism.[14] She writes, for example, "Community is almost always invoked as an unequivocal good, an indicator of a high quality of life, a life of human understanding, caring, selflessness, belonging … Among leftists and feminists, community has connoted cherished ideals of cooperation, equality and communion" (vii). Yet Zayas's representation of the female community reveals a more complex picture. The elite women who participate in these networks are required to participate in a strict policing of social norms. Their attitudes towards Fenisa also demonstrate a staunch antagonism towards difference.

In response to an excessively positive view of women's relations, Janet Halley has provocatively asked scholars to "take a break" from feminism in order to more closely examine the construction of community and its norms. Following Halley, this new critical lens allows scholars to better consider the ways in which certain feminine norms (collaboration, passivity) are celebrated, while displays of violence and aggression are strictly prohibited and punished. Although Zayas's *comedia* narrates the tale of a woman's betrayal of the female community, Joseph and Halley provide an alternative way to examine Fenisa's importance. Instead of interpreting Fenisa as merely "bad" in relation to her peers as an end point of analysis, scholars can utilize this critical

lens to examine how and why communities are formed. The study of
the disruptive vixen in relation to her larger community thus offers a
means of contextualizing early modern female power relations.

In its representation of the female community and the vixen who
disrupts the rules of sex and gender, Zayas's play depicts yet another
institution of containment for women who deviate from social norms.
As the title plainly suggests, Fenisa is a figure of betrayal. She openly
resists discretion, allegiance, friendship, monogamy, and restraint with
the aim of freely pursuing her own complex desires. For these reasons,
La traición depicts an elaborate representation of the underbelly of the
female community that provocatively parallel contemporary social
institutions designed for the containment of women. For scholars interested in uncovering the intricate history of female relations, it is necessary to resist the urge to relegate Fenisa to the corner of her text to
join with Zayas's cast in a celebration of marriage and the restoration
of order. Although it is tempting to project an idyllic representation of
women's community onto this institutionalized forgetfulness, to do so
would overlook the staggering and unsettling reality of women's relations during the period, which included not only monstrous displays
but also anomaly and difference.

4

Women's Exemplary Violence in Luis Vélez de Guevara's *La serrana de la Vera*

Luis Vélez de Guevara's *La serrana de la Vera* (The Mountain Girl of La Vera) (1613) narrates the tale of Gila, the amazon-like hunter turned man-hating murderess.[1] The play imbues new life into the mythical character of the sensuous mountain woman and recalls the classic tale of the *mujer varonil*, the betrayed woman, who takes on male dress to avenge her dishonour and marry.[2] In this story, however, Gila decides to reclaim her good name by killing every man with whom she comes into contact, a hefty sum that totals 2,000 men. Instead of marrying her unfaithful lover at the end of the play, as the traditional conclusion to the *mujer varonil* (masculine woman) script would dictate, Gila murders him and then is captured and killed for her crimes. Frequently referred to as Vélez de Guevara's only tragedy, the play asks its audience to consider the relationship between women, violence, and spectacle in the early modern period.[3]

Although in many ways *La serrana de la Vera* offers a novel representation of a powerful female character gone astray, its depiction of Gila puts the play into conversation with a number of other *comedias*. As C. George Peale explains, the play deals with the mythical "mountain woman" character and was likely a response to a play of the same title composed by Lope de Vega just years prior (260). The gender-bending protagonist is certainly influenced by a number of other contemporary plays. For example, in Lope's *El alcalde Mayor* (The Older Mayor), Rosarda's masculine disguise allows her to attend the University of Salamanca and become the mayor of Toledo until she decides to abandon her career and marry. The protagonists of Tirso de Molina's *Don Gil de las calzas verdes* (Don Gil of the Green Stockings) (Juana/Juan) and Ana Caro's *Valor, agravio y mujer* (Valour, Offence, and Woman) (Leonor/

Leonardo) utilize masculine disguise with the purpose of securing their own marriages. And finally, for its representation of a powerful ruler gone astray, the play is reminiscent of Calderón's depiction of Semíramis in *La hija del aire* (The Daughter of the Air). Most provocatively, the death sentence at the close of *La serrana* is one of many that feature a woman murdered for real or imagined transgressions, as in Calderón's trilogy of wife-murder plays. For example, the audiences are presented with Doña Mencía's corpse after her jealous husband bleeds her to death in order to protect his honour in *El medico de su honra* (The Physician of His Honour), and Anne Boleyn's corpse after Henry VIII beheads her in *La cisma de Inglaterra* (The Schism in England). The fact that the play closes with the display of Gila's corpse on stage is one of the earliest examples of an explicit staging of femicide, a transformative role in the *comedia* that gives rise to further female victims. Although some might argue that Gila's execution at the end of the play is fit punishment for her crimes, the play foregrounds numerous examples of violation of and violence against women that culminate in the final scene.

What makes Vélez de Guevara's depiction of the unruly protagonist even more unique is that he created his play to showcase the talents of one of the most famous actresses of his generation, Jusepa Vaca (b. 1600s–53).[4] As the daughter of playwright Juan Ruiz de Mendi and actress Mariana Vaca, Vaca was raised in the theatrical tradition and began to perform on stage at age seven. As Mercedes de los Reyes Peña relates, Vaca was married in 1602 to Juan de Morales Medrano, one of eight playwrights authorized by the king to travel and perform throughout Spain (83). Her daughter Mariana Vaca de Morales was baptized in Madrid in April 1608 and also joined the family theatre trade (Cotarelo y Mori, "Actores" 440n1). Stage directions attest to the playwright's praise of Vaca's acting ability, as for example in this note: "GILA poniéndole la escopeta a la vista, que lo hará muy bien la señora Jusepa" (Gila shows off the gun, as would do very well Sra. Jusepa) (Jornada I) (sd, act I).[5]

Vélez de Guevara was not the only dramatist taken with Vaca's performances. By 1615 Vaca was publically recognized by her contemporary Cristóbal Suárez de Figueroa as one of the "prodigiosas 'mujeres en representación' que España había tenido" (most prestigious actresses Spain had seen) (322v). Lope wrote another powerful female lead for the actress, the part of Doña Elvira (also betrayed by her family in the course of the play) in his play *Las almenas de toro* (The Bullfights) (1618). According to Hugo Rennert, Lope referred to the actress as "la gallarda" (striking) in the cast of characters, emphasizing the actress's physical charm. Additional praise for the actress can be found in the dedication of his play *Las Mocedades de Roldan* (Roldan's Mocedades) (1627), where Lope emphasizes Vaca's singular ability to play male characters "con la gracia de su accion, y la singularidad de su exemplo" (with the flair of her actions and the singularity of her example") (*La serrana* 155). Vaca's popularity undoubtedly contributed to the financial success of the production of *La serrana*. José Sánchez Arjona notes, for example, that in 1618 Vaca's company was awarded 10,200 maravedís "por joya y premio particular por lo bien que trabajaron en ... *La serrana de la Vera*" (as a reward and special prize for the great work in *The Mountain Girl of La Vera*) (120). She and her husband were commissioned together to direct various theatrical productions, as was the case in the example of the fiesta of Corpus de Sevilla in February 1616. The couple received 18,700 maravedís "por lo bien que parecieron a la ciudad en la representación que hicieron" (as acknowledgment from the city for the excellence of the performance) (Peña 86).

Vaca's fame seems to be as much about her abilities as an actress as the public's fascination with her real and imagined extramarital affairs with powerful men, including the Marqués de Villanueva and the Count-Duke of Olivares.[6] As Vaca stood at the familiar intersection between public adoration and censure, the question of whether or not she was a loyal wife was a favourite topic of playwrights, poets, and letter-writers of the period including Lope de Vega and Quevedo (Peña 91). As we recall from the introduction to this study, the early modern Spanish actress was already a literal site of contestation. Although she was critiqued as an embodiment of sin and illness her popularity generated the revenue to fund charitable projects designed to promote health and virtue. As the suspect actress played the righteous heroine, she was marked at once for the entertainment value of her sexuality as well as for the exemplary status of her chaste performance.

Vaca's popularity as an actress even complicates the simple categorization of the play's genre.[7] While the plot's violent end and cautionary undertones have traditionally favoured the Aristotelian category of tragedy, I argue that because this play was designed specifically for this famous actress, there is a significant impact on the way it was broadcast to its audience. In a time when the mere presence of women on stage elicited a variety of critiques, Vélez de Guevara's choice to cast one of Spain's most controversial actresses certainly impacts the impression and consequences of his play's reception. Because the play's lead character was written for an actress noted for her comic appeal, chiefly her bold excess and seductive charms, it is important to take note of the ways *La serrana de la Vera* can also be read as a comedy. This fusion of both dramatic genres calls to mind Francisco de Cascales's provocative description of contemporary Spanish tragicomic plays as *hermafroditos* (hermaphrodites) and *monstruos de la poesía* (poetic monsters) in his 1617 *Tablas poéticas* (Poetic Tables).

In this way, as much as Vaca, her fictional counterpart, and the monstrous genre she represented can be read as models to avoid; they can also be understood as a celebrated example of achievement. In the economic context of the theatre at the least, Vélez de Guevara's choice of heroines offered a successful model of *comedia* that used the talents of one of Madrid's most beloved actresses in order to create a box office hit. Gila's dominating presence on stage was profitable, captivating, and often very funny. With these contrasting representations in mind, this chapter asks: How does the spectacle of Vaca/Gila's body achieve an effect that is both comedic and cautionary? What are the observers of Vélez de Guevara's play meant to learn through the staging of punishment at the close of the play?

The audience first witnesses Gila on stage as she arrives dramatically on horseback and is received with a chorus of adulatory songs. Her show-stopping entrance marks her from the start of the play for her celebrated excess and pushes her qualities as entertainer to the forefront. It is therefore a surprise when her father proceeds to remark: "¡Que edades / sin fin vivas para *ejemplo* / de mujeres españolas!" (That you should live for ages on end as an *example* to Spanish women!) (Vélez de Guevara 255–7, emphasis mine), stressing the protagonist's exemplarity, which runs counter to the social norms set for women's behaviour in public. As the play opens in a topsy-turvy world of excess, daughters are most humorously praised by their fathers for their dramatic appeal.

From the first scene forward, Vélez de Guevara's play adheres to the logic of the *comedia de enredo* (comedy of errors), which features prominently the antics of its exemplary protagonist. Gila is repeatedly praised for her masculine strength and valour and early on wins the coveted attention of Don Lucas. When the heroine is betrayed by her lover, Vélez de Guevara departs significantly and suddenly from the typical formula of the *comedia*. Instead of following the rules assigned to the *mujer varonil*, Gila vows to take revenge and murder every man with whom she comes into contact until she can find and kill Don Lucas. In a radical exaggeration of the limits of transgression normally allowed to the character type, Gila's murderous rampage dominates the stage and powerfully illustrates the reach of both her feminine charm and her masculine prowess.[8]

In parallel to Gila's entrance at the start of the play, where Giraldo names his daughter an "example," at the play's end Gila's body is again put on display. Gila is punished for her crimes and her corpse on stage is described as "una memoria / que de ejemplo sirva a España" (a memory that will serve as an example to Spain) (3296–7). The question of how to understand Gila's story frequently lends itself to an interpretation of the play in terms of a cautionary tale. Giraldo as the misguided father has poorly instructed his naturally weak-minded daughter and has failed to counsel her with the advice of contemporary conduct manuals. Because he wrongfully celebrated her at the play's opening, he is punished by her death at the play's end. But Gila's forceful presence on stage, principally the novel staging of her violence as well as the comedic force of her excess, complicates this kind of didactic reading. To liberate Gila from the frame of the cautionary tale is to open the space to consider the shifting meanings of exemplarity throughout the play. Reading *La serrana de la Vera* through this lens – with particular attention to the display of Gila and Vaca's body – it is possible to explore how the playwright problematizes and exacerbates the tension between the subject she attempts to be and the object she sometimes becomes.

Gila's exemplary status is evident from her first appearance on stage, at the centre of a parade created in her honour. Replete with elaborate costume and music, the celebration honours Gila's hunting prowess. She enters on horseback, adorned with feathers and weaponry: "vestida a lo serrano de muger, con sayuelo y muchas patenas, el cabello tendido y una montera con plumas, un cuchillo de monte al lado, botín argentado y puesta una escopeta debaxo del caparazón del caballo" (dressed as a mountain girl, with a decorated smock, tied hair and a feathered cap, a mountain knife at her side, silver boots and a gun underneath the horse's saddle) (sd 77–8). The townspeople praise her valour and strength through song and honour her distinctiveness through repetition of the following verse: "¡Quién como ella, / la serrana de la Vera!" (Who is like her, the Mountain Girl of the Vera!) (205–6). Gila's entrance is reminiscent of parallel religious processions for feast days and Holy Week in Seville and other Spanish cities, where women "became significant symbols of local pride and religious strength" (Perry, *Gender* 36).

Certainly, the way the scene is set positions Gila as a site of veneration and celebrates her independence.

The opening scene also recalls the tale of the Spanish actress and author Ana Muñoz (b. 1588?), well known for her cross-dressed performances. Melveena McKendrick recounts the following anecdote where the pregnant actress entered the stage dressed as a man and on horseback. The audience so applauded her entrance that they startled her horse, which bolted and caused the premature birth of her child (*Theatre in Spain* 197). Although the story seems an implausible coincidence, the anecdote reveals contemporary anxieties about women who play men on stage. Here the Spanish actress conceivably represented to great acclaim the part of a powerful man. The fact that she was no longer able to sustain the illusion of the play when she birthed her child on stage repositioned her to a less transgressive social category as the clearly identifiable role of mother. The detail of the audience's applause as what incited the birthing scene is yet another compelling dimension of the story, as it explicitly limits the actress's talent for gender bending and makes obvious the material realities of her birthing body. Perhaps a contemporary adaptation of biblical explanations of childbirth, Muñoz appeared to have given birth on stage as a consequence for her wrongdoings.

In the first act of the play, Gila's father Giraldo celebrates his daughter's unmatched strength and valour. Playing the roles of both father and agent, Giraldo speaks praises of his daughter:

> una hija me dio el zielo
> que podré decir que vale
> por dos hijos, / ... /
> tan gran valor
> tiene, que no hay labrador
> en la Vera de Plasencia
> que a correr no desafíe,
> a saltar, luchar, tirar
> tienen ya gran experiencia
> que es su ardimiento biçarro

> Heaven gave me a daughter that you may say is worth at least two sons ... she has such great valour that there is not a young man in la Vera of Plasencia that she wouldn't challenge with her experience in running, jumping, fighting, throwing, which is her courageous valour. (Vélez de Guevara 129–30, 134–46)

Giraldo unconventionally honours his daughter as worth at least two sons. He describes her as unmatched in a variety of traditionally masculine arts and emphasizes how Gila is held up as a model throughout la Vera de Plasencia. Gila is constantly on display for both the instruction and entertainment of her town. In her hunting exploits, for example, a large crowd of supporters cheers her on. The scene depicts both the huntress celebrated by her townspeople as well as the actress surrounded by her fans: "y casi todo el lugar tras ella, que la siguió / siempre que a caza ha salido, / por verla con la escopeta" (with nearly the whole town behind her, following her each time she hunts to see her with the gun) (159–62). Admired not only for her hunting ability, she also draws attention because of her anomalous status: she is a woman with a gun.

Gila is praised alternately for her beauty and her strength, characteristics typically cast as opposites for the romantic heroine of the *comedia*. In the opening scene, for example, when she is celebrated for her hunting victories, detail is paradoxically paid to her physical charms rather than her physical strength: "ojos hermosos rasgados / la serrana de la Vera; / lisa frente, roxos labios, / la serrana de la Vera; / pelo de ámbar, blancas manos / la serrana de la Vera; / cuerpo genzor y adamado" (beautiful almond-shaped eyes / The Mountain Girl of La Vera / smooth brow, red lips / The Mountain Girl of La Vera / amber hair, white hands / The Mountain Girl of La Vera / an elegant and delicate body) (213–20). As in the story of Ana Muñoz, Gila's femininity is often emphasized as a contrast to her masculinity.

In another example, the townspeople voice their desire for Gila to marry and become a mother:

Dios mil años nos la guarde
la serrana de la Vera,
y la dé un galán amante,
la serrana de la Vera,
para que con ella case
la serrana de la Vera,
y para a los doze pares

May she be protected for 2000 years, The Mountain Girl of La Vera, and awarded a handsome young lover, the Mountain Girl of La Vera, so that she may marry, the Mountain Girl of La Vera, and have twelve children. (235–41)

The townspeople describe the future of Gila's motherhood nearly as excessively as her present standing – not simply a mother, but a mother of twelve. Here feminine norms are overstated with the aim of matching her current excess. As it is precarious for Gila to be such a prominent single woman, marriage and motherhood are offered in this chorus as solutions for her social integration. Further, the playwright makes reference to the legendary "doce pares" (twelve knights) of King Arthur's round table with its stories of heroism and, more important, betrayal.

Despite these pressures, Gila resists identification as a woman in need of containment. This is especially true in interactions among Gila, Don Lucas, and her father. Stage directions draw attention to her masculinity, as Gila is instructed to dismount from her horse and visibly take hold of her gun. It is in fact this masculinity that initially attracts Don Lucas, as he exclaims: "De puro admirado callo. / No he visto en hombre jamás / tan varonil biçarría" (I am silenced by pure admiration / I have never before seen in a man such manly valour) (248–50). Likewise, Gila's father is awestruck by his daughter's appearance and claims that she is a model for other women: "¡Qué edades / sin fin vivas, para exemplo / de mugeres españolas!" (That you should live for ages on end as an example to Spanish women!) (255–7). Gila also asserts her masculinity through speech. For example, she challenges the advances of Don Lucas when she proclaims, "Si imagináis / que lo soy, os engañáis, / que soy muy hombre" (If you imagine that I am, you are tricked, as I am very much a man) (350–2). When Gila claims that she is very manly, she expresses her distaste for female norms and expectations.

Gila is depicted as a most enticing love interest because she is difficult to dominate. Garzía once again cites the conflation of her beauty and strength as he points out Gila to Don Lucas: "tiene en la Vera notable fama de hermosa / y de muger valerosa" (she has in la Vera notable fame as a brave and beautiful woman) (471–2). Once she has been identified as a challenge worthy of his strength, Don Lucas speedily vows to dominate Gila as if capturing new territory in war: "Hazed sacar la bandera / de la villa, don Garzía, / que mexor será en Plasencia / levantalla, y con violencia / de toda una campañía / abrasar este lugar / y gozar esta muger / tan brava" (Take out the flag of the town, Don Garzía, for Plasencia will be better off when I, with violence and a whole campaign, set fire to this land and plunder this fierce woman) (474–81). To tame and conquer the fierce *mujer varonil* along with the spoils of her land thus motivates Don Lucas's overtures, contrasting Gila's honourable strength with Don Lucas's brute masculinity. Don

Lucas's warlike mindset can be most clearly appreciated right after he seduces and betrays Gila, when he claims: "Yo llegué, engañé y venzí" (I came, I tricked and I conquered) (995).

At the end of the first act Gila is once more celebrated for her physical strength as she enters another masculine circle – she expertly tames a bull in front of a huge crowd. Reminiscent of Lope de Vega's *Caballero de Olmedo* (The Knight from Olmedo) (1620) in action as a display of heroism in medieval games, Gila manages to shock the audience merely because she is a woman who undertakes the task. When one onlooker exclaims, "¿Una mujer / toma la espada?" (A woman takes the sword?) (725–6), Gila cleverly replies: "Muger sóy sólo en la saya" (I am only a woman in my smock) (773). As she prepares to begin the bullfight, Gila stands at the centre of the ring and delivers an extended monologue to the eager crowd. She emphatically characterizes herself as a fierce match for the bull when, for example, she proclaims, "con la serrana os tomáis; / con la que a brazo partido / mata al osso, al jabalí" (You are taken with the Mountain Girl, who with a broken arm kills the bear, the wild boar) (838–40).

The speed and ferocity with which Gila tames the bull is almost comical given the circumstances. Not merely a crossed-dressed woman who tricks her lover into a marriage proposal, here Gila's masculine embodiment reaches new heights. She creates a literal theatre for herself, in which she casts herself as heroine at the centre of the crowd-packed bullring. Without hesitation Gila dominates and conquers her match. Although the scene would not have been staged, one of the king's servants, Nuño delivers a captivating and emotional account of the scene, likely to have provoked a titillated response from the audience, at once awed by Gila's superhuman strength and enticed by her prohibited power. As Nuño describes it, "por los cuernos asió ya / al toro feroz, y agora / le rinde como si fuera / una oveja" (She has grabbed the horns of the fierce bull, and now she subdues him as if he were a sheep) (925–8). At the end of the bullfight, Gila and Don Lucas are cast in expert opposition to each other, as each engages in precise acts of domination to assert their strength.

This bullfighting scene also explores Gila's relationship with one very important audience member: Queen Isabel.[9] When her cousin Madalena asks if she feels distracted by the crowds of men in the audience (625–6), Gila replies that she is only focused on the attention of the queen: "Rabiando vengo por ver / a la reina, porque délla, / después de dezir que es bella, / dizen que es brava muger" (I come

ravenously to see the queen, because when they speak of her, after saying she is beautiful they say she is a fierce woman) (631–4). The presence of Fernando and Isabel as historical markers to this play should
not be underestimated, especially considering the famous motto of the
Spanish monarchs, which spoke to their projected image of equality:
"Tanto monta, monta tanto, Isabel como Fernando" (They amount to
the same).[10] Gila is not interested in impressing the crowd, but focuses
her attention exclusively on Isabel, emphasizing their shared characteristics. Her admiration for the queen is what ultimately convinces Gila
to accept Don Lucas's marriage offer, not out of love but out of imita-
tion: "Esa razón me puede obligar sola, / por imitar a vuestro lado
luego / a la gran Isabel" (This reason may alone convince me, to imitate
by your side the great Isabel) (1612–14). Gila agrees to marry with two
goals in mind: to bolster her own image and to fulfil a dutiful obligation
to the model role she plays for her own community.

The proposed marriage between Gila and Don Lucas is fraught with
conflict from the start. When Don Lucas first asks Giraldo for his daughter's hand in marriage, Giraldo points out the inequality of the match,
and characterizes his daughter as "labradora, hija de un hombre /
llano y humilde, aunque de limpia sangre" (a labourer, daughter of a
plain and humble man, although of clean blood) (1486–7).[11] Yet Don Lucas claims he is interested in Gila not because she is a socially appropriate match but because of her fame and reputation: "¿qué madre mexor
puedo a mis hijos / darles que una muger que es tan famosa?" (What
better mother could I offer my children than such a famous woman?)
(1504–5). Because the two men agree on Gila's unusual status, an agreement is made. Again the play celebrates the protagonist's anomalous
qualities.

In contrast, Gila criticizes the offer and pokes fun at Don Lucas's no-
bility and claims she deserves someone with an even higher social rank:
"¿He heredado las casas, las haziendas / de los señores de Castilla? ...
¿Llámanme para h[az]erme prencipessa / de Castilla y León?" (Have
I inherited the homes and estates of the lords of Castile? ... Are they
calling me to name me princess of Castile y León?) (1557–61). Gila's
humorous complaint serves to bolster her own image. She also claims
she lacks the proper education to assume the role of wife but instead
excels at being a man. "Hasta agora / me imaginaba, padre, por las
cosas / que yo me he visto h[az]er, hombre y muy hombre; / y agora
echo de ver, pues que me tratas / casamiento con este caballero, / que
soy muger" (Until now, Father, I have imagined myself a man, for the

manly things that I have seen myself do, and now I have just seen, as you try to marry me with this man, that I am a woman) (1578–83). Gila emphasizes that marriage to Don Lucas will undermine the hard work she and her father have undertaken that has rendered her successful and exemplary in so many arenas. She continues:

> No me quiero casar, padre, que creo
> que mientras no me caso que soy hombre.
> No quiero ver que nadie me sujete,
> no quiero que ninguno se imagine
> dueño de mí; la libertad pretendo.
> El señor capitán busque en Plasencia
> muger de su nobleza que le iguale,
> que yo soy una triste labradora
> muy diferente dêl, / ... /
> no quiero
> meterme agora a caballera y h[az]erme
> muger de piedra en lo espetado y tiesso,
> encaramada en dos chapines, padre / ... /
> y Gila no es buen nombre para doña.

I do not want to marry, Father, as I think that while I do not marry I am a man. I do not want to see anyone hold me down. I don't want anyone to imagine that they are my owner. I expect my liberty. The captain should look in Plasencia for a noble woman of his equal, as I am a sad working girl, very different from him ... I do not want to pair myself with this gentleman and be transformed into a woman of stone, stiff and stern, made tall in high heels, Father ... and Gila is not a good match for Mrs. (1584–1601)

While she initially cites their differences in background and social status, ultimately Gila argues that marriage will destroy her independence and liberty. She also maintains that marriage reinforces her status as a woman and thus renders her and her family name more vulnerable. She compares men's and women's dress, and again stresses their differences in liberties as well as the idea that she could not be her true self in women's clothes. Throughout her monologue, Gila criticizes the conventions of marriage, but concludes on a comic note. Through the simple statement that even her name is not fit for marriage, Gila undercuts the seriousness of her monologue with the humorous frivolity of her final complaint.

Although Gila's status as an exemplary figure is apparent throughout the play, her response to her abandonment by Don Lucas is a pivotal moment for the play.[12] In the middle of act 2, Gila draws attention to her dishonour through a series of fragmented exclamations that call to mind parallel betrayals, as, for example, Tisbea's in *El burlador de Sevilla*: "¡Traición! ¡Traición! ¡Padre! ¡Prima! / ¡Mingo! ¡Pascual! ¡Antón! ... / ¡Ah de mi casa! ¡Ah del pueblo! / ¡Qué se me van con mi honor; / que un ingrato caballero / me lleva el alma! ¡Socorro!" (Betrayal! Betrayal! Father! Cousin! Mingo! Pascual! Antón! ... Oh my home! Oh my village! That this ungrateful gentleman has taken my honour along with my soul! Help!) (2050–6). Gila again recognizes the importance of her own exemplarity as she links her personal betrayal and ruptured honour with her family name and the larger community of Plasencia. She attributes her ruin not only to Don Lucas, but to her brief lapse as a frailer woman: "que no hay muger que resista / en mirando y en oyendo. / Como imaginé que estaba / tan cercano el casamiento, / le di esta noche en mis brazos / ocasión para ofenderos" (There is not a woman who would resist in seeing and listening. As I imagined our marriage night was so close, tonight I gave in my arms an occasion to offend) (2094–9). As she recognizes her obligation to Plasencia, Gila virtuously takes responsibility for her own betrayal and vows to avenge her dishonour.

Motivated by this newfound sense of duty, Gila is patently transformed. She is characterized by her ferocity but is also marked by her piety. This unexpected fusion further reinforces her connection to Queen Isabel, the prime example in this tenuous yet effective combination. Likewise, it recalls the explicit combination of religious and penal discourse that characterized the custodial institutions of the time. Immediately after her betrayal, Gila vows the following to her father:

si a mi enemigo no alcanzo,
que hasta matarlo no pienso
dexar hombre con la vida;
y hago al zielo juramento
de no volver a poblado,
de no peinarme el cabello,
de no dormir desarmada,
de comer siempre en el suelo
sin manteles, y de andar
siempre al agua, al sol y al viento,
sin que me acobarde el día

If I do not reach my enemy, until I kill him I will not leave one man with his life. And I swear to the heavens to not return to the village, to not brush my hair, to not sleep unarmed, to always eat on the ground without table-cloths and to walk always through water, sun, and wind without letting the day unnerve me. (2136–46)

Gila's promise of violent revenge is the most noteworthy element of this scene, yet it is also important for how she rejects the amenities and comfort of the material world. She chooses to be a single woman and to live in poverty. She embodies a life of hardship and rejects vanity and luxury for a life dedicated to revenge. Although she is eventually punished for her wrongdoings, this austere behaviour complicates the treatment of her transgressions and fall.

In the closing act of the play, the audience finally witnesses Gila as murderess. True to her promise, Gila kills nearly every man with whom she comes into contact, although the audience only witnesses a handful of her murders on stage.[13] Gila both sanctifies and dehumanizes her victim, fusing staging and confession in a style well-loved by the *auto de fé*: "Esta cruz te debo; tenga / el cielo de ti piedad" (I give you this cross, may the heavens have mercy on you) (2263–4). Gila repeats a nearly identical crime later in the third act with Andrés, who opens the scene with an extensive survey of the *serrana*'s beauty (2795–805). This time, Andrés goes so far as to ask, "¿Dormís sola, linda cara?" (Do you sleep alone, lovely face?) (2816) and thus instigates his speedy demise as Gila hurls him off the mountain (2842).

When King Fernando invades Gila's territory in the middle of the act, the audience witnesses a novel side of the protagonist as murder-ess. At the start of the scene it is obvious that the king initially fears for his life, and forcefully demands space (2529). Much to his surprise, Gila explains that he is free from her wrath because he is in fact not a man. In her words:

Por satisfazer la ofensa
de un hombre, y hasta matalle
he prosupuesto que mueran
con solemne juramento / ... /
y no quiebro el juramento,
que el rey es Dios en la tierra,
y en lugar suyo, Fernando,
la justicia representas.
Y pues no eres hombre, voy

In order to satisfy the offence of one man through his death, I suppose all
should die with solemn oath. And I will not break the oath for the king is
God of the land, and as is your place, Fernando, you represent justice. And
since you are not a man, I will go. (2557–68)

Gila's explanation offers another justification for her murders as well
as a definition for men that inscribes them as a group for their ability to
provoke injustice and harm. Because Fernando is a just ruler according
to Gila, she qualifies him as exempt from her revenge. In fact, by protecting Fernando from harm, she imagines herself in allegiance with Isabel. As the motto of the monarchs recalls, "Tanto monta, monta tanto,
Isabel como Fernando," it is no wonder that Gila protects Fernando in
honour of her love for Isabel. In both of these scenes, Gila's brutality is
mediated by her intelligence and sense of justice.

When Pascuala visits Gila, the audience is able to observe how the
protagonist's image and reputation has changed for her beloved town
of Plasencia. No longer a celebrated hero, Gila is described as a savage
monster. Again Gila reminds Pascuala of the logic of her actions: "¿No
os satisfaze / que sólo mi furor haze / mal a los hombres aquí / y que a las
mugeres no? / Que el que he de satisfacer / es agravio de muger, / y soy la
ofendida yo" (Are you not satisfied that only my fury does wrong to the
men here and not to women? What I need to avenge is the offence of a
woman and I am the offended one) (2675–81), once more pointing the
audience to the specificity of her rage and the cause of her offence. But
Pascuala, along with the townspeople she represents, will not be easily
swayed. In sharp contrast to the opening of the play, they now characterize her in stark terms: "Locifer, / saltabardales, machorra, / ... /
el lobo de sus ovexas, / de sus gallinas la zorra" (Lucifer, mischief
maker, sterile woman ... the wolf of the sheep, the fox of the chickens)
(2697–701). It is valuable here to consider the accusation of Gila as a
sterile woman. In contrast to the first act of the play where the townspeople imagine her as glorious Gila, mother of a mythical twelve, the
idea of her sterility functions as an affront to both her femininity and
her legendary status. The insult is perhaps one of the most violent accusations made against her and reveals yet again the multiple valences
inherent in the protagonist.

Considering that Gila's final murder scene comes directly after this
conversation with Pascuala, the way in which Gila chooses to handle
herself with Don Lucas serves as a test: Will Gila be characterized by
her rationality and piousness or merely by her brutality? When Don

Lucas enters the scene, he is described much like the earlier travellers. Belittling his own ability and ambition, Don Lucas seeks assistance from Gila, and repeatedly emphasizes that he is lost and is in need of aid (2945–51). When he later tries to convince Gila of his romantic eligibility by wooing her (of course he does not recognize Gila for who she is), she is quick to call him out for his lies:

Mentís, que hay testigo aquí
de que verdades no habláis.
Yo soy Gila, a quien estáis
deudor de tan justa quexa,
que el delito os aconsexa
lo mismo que vos huís

You lie, there is a witness here to claim that you are not telling the truth. I am Gila, to whom you are indebted for a just complaint. I tell of this offence at the same time as you flee. (3038–43)

Gila directly accuses Don Lucas of lying, identifies herself as a witness, and reiterates his lack of truthfulness. She goes on to reassert her status as victim and remind him of his crimes.

The legalistic quality of her language prompts yet another shock in the scene, when Don Lucas, fearing for his own life, again proposes marriage: "Gila, palabra te di / de ser tu esposo. Aquí estoy: / tu esposo y tu esclavo soy" (Gila, I give you my word to be your husband. Here I am, your husband and slave) (3066–8). Gila defies the expected norm of the masculine woman character type who would initially resist but then accede and she rejects the marriage offer as she claims, "Ya es tarde, ingrato" (It is too late, you ingrate) (3069). Brute anger prevails over the expected logic of the scene, where the Golden Age heroine typically forgives all past betrayals in exchange for the marriage vow. Instead, Gila reiterates that Don Lucas needs to pay directly for her unrecoverable honour: "quien tal haze, que tal pague" (He who acts must pay) (3074). Reworking the honour drama formula in which the man cleanses his own dishonour (real or suspected) by murdering his wife, Gila murders Don Lucas with the intention of recovering her good name.

Not surprisingly, Gila's community of Plasencia resists her new adaptation of the honour code. The crowd's responses explicitly represent a popularized and institutional persecution of a female criminal. Her

father, up until this point consistently represented as a staunch sup-
porter of his daughter, is the first to condemn her: "Tú eres hija de ese
pecho / cruel, que no pude yo / engendrarte" (You are the daughter
of a cruel body, I could not have made you) (3092–4). Giraldo comes to
the mountaintop to bring his daughter to jail, accompanied by an army
of men. Without hesitation Gila accepts her handcuffs and chains and
hands over her weapons to her father. She states simply that she has
achieved her goal and reminds the audience of her betrayal: "Vengué,
en efeto, mi honor" (I have avenged my honour) (3116).

Gila's crimes and merits are even a topic of conversation between
Fernando and Isabel. After he weighs the protagonist's merits and
wrongdoings, the king ultimately suggests that her crimes deserve
harsh punishment:

> Castiguen como es justo a los ladrones,
> sin que haya apelación, que dêsta suerte
> se evitarán muy grandes ocasiones,
> fuera de que ésta ha dado a muchos muerte
> y la mereze por razón de estado

> Punish her as you would justly punish thieves, without appeal, as
> in this manner you will avoid many grave occasions, as this one has
> caused many deaths and deserves her punishment by reason of the state.
> (3167–71)

Fernando's quick punishment of Gila reinforces inscribed boundaries for women's behaviour. While perhaps a spectacle of strength like
the one she exerted at the bullfight fell within appropriate exhibitory
norms, Gila's rewritten honour code is simply not tolerable. The visible
extremity of Gila's punishment suggests that she has overstepped her
bounds. Gila is punished for her wrongful crimes and the display of her
body reminds the audience not to follow her path. Yet Isabel also remarks, "Pena me ha dado, / sabiendo que es muger" (It causes me grief
knowing that she is a woman) (3174–5): her comment reflects tensions
in regard to the gendering of violence. The queen evinces her sympathy
with Gila, understanding – as Vélez makes clear – that a woman's role
in male-dominated society is always fraught.

This final scene offers an alternate and more explicit explanation for
Gila's weaknesses when she blames her father for her unfortunate status. Gila asks her father to come closer, apparently to permit her one last

opportunity to lament her woes or whisper confessions to her forgiving father. When her mouth reaches her father's ear, Gila surprises the crowd again and viciously challenges the expected convention when she bites off his ear. She insists that her violent actions are exemplary:

esto mereze quien pasa
por las libertades todas
de los hijos. Si tú usaras
rigor conmigo al principio
de mi inclinación gallarda,
yo no llegara a este extreme

This is what he deserves who allows all liberties to his children. If you had used rigour to curb my brave inclination, I would not have arrived at this extreme. (3251–6)

Here Gila explicitly ridicules the negligent or indulgent father as she threatens parents to instruct their children well as a means to avoid the extreme behaviour she has enacted, while she serves as comedic relief through her dramatic excess. The behaviour of both the father and the daughter may come as a surprise to the audience as it strongly contrasts with the close relationship the two have shared up until the final scene. While it would be punishment enough for Gila to lose her life at the expense of her father's misdeeds, the fact that she circumvents expectations to showcase her own excess again speaks to the complex relationship the play has with entertaining its crowds. With this scene Vélez de Guevara differentiates his play from the standard cautionary tale and crafts a signature dramatic moment that marks his actress as legendary and leaves his audience awestruck.

Despite the ear biting, Gila still manages to reassert her piety in the final moments of the scene. In her final monologue, for example, she emulates female martyrs and expresses a sense of contentment and tranquility.[14] Instead of protesting a wrongful punishment, Gila simply states that she is, "contenta muero por ver / que el cielo, con ésta, traza / de mi predestinación / el bien que mi muerte aguarda" (I die content seeing that the heavens with this design of my predestination, awaits my death) (3230–3). Following the standard depiction of conversion posited by the *comedia* and practised in the ceremonial *auto de fe*, Gila freely confesses her crimes from the past: "por estas manos ingratas/ tengo a cargo dos mil vidas, / de que pido perdón" (With these ingrate hands, I bear the responsibility of two thousand lives, for which I beg forgiveness) (3240–2). When she admits her actions and accepts her fate, Gila's Christ-like death sentence produces an overwhelming response of sympathy in her audience. Even though Gila's father is blamed for not properly instructing his daughter, ultimately she is the one who fatally suffers.

Once she has been killed, Gila's body is compared directly to St Sebastian's (3276), staunch defender of Christianity and patron saint of soldiers: "corren el tafetán, y parezca GILA en el palo, arriba, llena de saetas y el cabello sobre el rostro" (the curtain opens and Gila appears on the stick, above, her body pricked with arrows and her face covered with her hair) (sd 204). At once sensual and grotesque, the final scene produces what Richard Rambuss has termed a "devotional homoerotics" in which devotion is viewed as a form of desire.[15] Both as its own event and as a replication of the religious narrative, Fernando solemnly proclaims that Gila's body serves as an example to Spain: "quedando allí una memoria / que de exemplo sirva a España" (leaving a memory here that will serve as an example to Spain) (1139–40). But what does this model represent?

Fernando's pronouncement cements the multifaceted interrelationship between violence, spectacle, and exemplarity that pervades not only Vélez de Guevara's play but also the culture of the period where public displays of punishment, religiosity, and penitence were a common factor of daily life. With its enactment of Gila's execution at the close of the play, Vélez de Guevara explicitly depicts and most suggestively stages an execution that closely mimics the contemporary techniques of the *auto de fe*. But the play does more than merely copy a captivating social phenomenon. It exploits the rarity of the real-life *auto* to provide audiences with the pleasure and satisfaction of witnessing such acute public display on demand. Violence is the major topic of this *comedia*, most prominently seen in the murders that Gila commits and her execution, but also in real and symbolic violence enacted against the non-normative woman in her betrayal by her lover, her townspeople, and her father.

As the audience members witness the execution of Plasencia's beloved *serrana*, consider that they also witness the execution of Madrid's beloved actress, Jusepa Vaca. The scene at once exploits Vaca's life of romantic excess while it showcases her sensuous body. While it would seem that such a violent display would quickly alienate the audience, instead it produced the opposite response. Gila's audacity, excess, and challenge to social norms once again shock and delight her audience; they serve at once to critique and uphold contested social norms. Performing exemplary violence thus serves as the backdrop for the space of theatrical desire, where the spectacle of the unruly woman's body produces a runaway success. As exemplary figures, Gila and Vaca should be characterized by their extremity: strikingly beautiful, fierce, and certainly captivating. And yet what is unique about the play and the actress it features is the sheer violence it permits to its heroine, as she reworks the honour code and kills 2,000 men in the process. Gila's violence – one that is transparent and whose agency she fully claims – leaves its own exemplary mark on the audience of the play. *La serrana de la Vera* demands a revision of traditional norms that punish women for exerting their power and, worse yet, for making a scene.

Conclusion

Although the execution scene provided dramatic closure to Luis Vélez de Guevara's *La serrana de la Vera*, Jusepa Vaca, the actress who inspired the play, was reborn at the end of each curtain call. Time and again, the dramatic world celebrated the actress's readiness to enact Gila's independence, transgressions, and fall in another performance. Vaca enjoyed success on stage; she was widely celebrated for her ability to take on masculine roles in Vélez de Guevara's play and many others, yet her powerful reputation in society continued to be a favourite subject of conversation. As the satirical poet Count of Villamediana, Juan de Tassis y Peralta famously advised the actress, brazenly assuming the poetic voice of her husband: "Oiga, Josefa, y mire que ya pisa / esta corte del rey, cordura tenga; / mire que el vulgo en murmurar se venga / y el tiempo siempre sin hablar avisa" (Listen, Josefa, now that you already walk all over the king's court, act with common sense; / Look how the masses avenge with their whispers, and how time, without speaking, advises) (269).

As he highlights the social and political advantage her romance provided, the poet cautions the actress not to overstep her already fragile position, a succinct and severe signal of the importance of discretion in Vaca's personal life. She is harshly counselled to "act sensibly" in her own life, although her performance on stage was never questioned. Francisco de Quevedo also made Vaca an object of satire in his poem *Diálogo entre Morales y Josepa, que había sido honrada cuando moza y vieja dio en mala mujer* (Dialogue between Morales and Josepa, who had been honourable when she was young, and as an old lady became a bad woman) the actress is depicted as decrepit and vulgar. By and large, Jusepa Vaca's part in theatre society (where she is accepted) and her role in the wider culture (where her actions if not her very existence are questioned) are brought into dynamic confrontation. These tensions and contradictions – among independence, entertainment, and innovation, and control, punishment, and exclusion – stand as emblems for the essence and problematics of the lived and perceived deviance of women and the portrayed deviance of women on stage.

The presence of non-normative women on stage in the Spanish *comedia* offers both support and critique for the traditional values that dictate and produce the standards for significant issues in women's lives. This critical examination of three prominent character types for women – the widow, the vixen, and the murderess – demonstrates the ways in which a variety of popular playwrights, both men and women, comment on women's non-normative relationships to the topics of marriage, sex, and violence as well as the overlaps between them. The shape-shifting widow Ángela in Pedro Calderón de la Barca's *La dama duende* (1629), the back-stabbing girlfriend Fenisa in María de Zayas's *La traición en la amistad* (1630), and the amazon-like hunter turned man-hating murderess Gila in Luis Vélez de Guevara's *La serrana de la Vera* (1613) have in common the fact that they defy the rules assigned to their gender. The distinct character types and rehabilitative strategies depicted by each of these playwrights in representative ways provide a framework for contextualizing the plays.

Each playwright communicates a unique narrative of rehabilitation to the audience: Ángela's happy marriage, Fenisa's exclusion from marriage, and Gila's exemplary murder. Although they vary widely in seriousness and tone, the outcome assigned to each heroine provides a means to discern the play's moral code, where the severity of the end of each play matches the gravity of the crime. In *La dama duende* and *La traición en la amistad*, rehabilitation is depicted as both a practice of containment and protection for women. Although Ángela circumvents the rules assigned to her by her brothers, she does not deviate far outside of the social norm. She is able to have her needs met at the end of the play in the happy resolution of the male-negotiated marriage. In *La traición en la amistad*, exemplary women are likewise rewarded with marriage for their good conduct while the deviant Fenisa is cast out from her community. Still, the case of *La serrana de la Vera*'s exemplary murder at the end of the play troubles this framework of rehabilitation and moves more explicitly into a discussion of punishment.

Part of the appeal of these dramatic works and the heroines that they represent is that they play off contemporary cultural values about what is and is not possible for women. Although these *comedias* follow the standard structure of the three-act play, which concludes with a scene of marriage or death, these dramatic works also demonstrate the *process* of rehabilitation, not simply the outcome. Thus, the dramatic rehabilitative solutions proposed by these plays alone do not offer a definitive frame for the contextualization of women's behaviour. Rehabilitation for women is based on the assumption that it is possible to renegotiate one's status in ways that do not necessarily fit neatly within dramatic categories and resolutions. Early modern practices of rehabilitation imply a more fluid negotiation of status in ways that frequently disrupt the clear social categories used to describe their outcomes: married or single, comic or tragic. Similarly, the study of rehabilitative practices enacted by contemporary custodial institutions cannot be limited to a study of outcomes alone, but rather should focus on the multiple and frequently contradictory practices of rehabilitation for women. The comparison between these real and fictional accounts of women's rehabilitation should make evident and explicit their differences, even if it is tempting to read narratives of rehabilitation with an eye towards clean dramatic closure.

In early modern Spain unruly women played starring roles not only in the public theatre but also in Madrid's custodial institutions, where the drama of gender-specific punishment took centre stage. Through an analysis of the rehabilitation narratives displayed in the *comedias*, readers can begin to appreciate the ways in which public performance also infused (monetarily and systematically) the institutional and spiritual practices of *recogimiento* enacted by contemporary custodial institutions. Madrid was newly designed around the concept of shared public spaces for the purpose of projecting a clear sense of social order, which most famously occurred through the ceremonial *auto*. Custodial institutions of the period were likewise impacted by exemplary public displays.

Both inside and outside of their institutional confines and through the implementation of varied objectives, La Casa de Santa María Magdalena de la Penitencia and Madre Magdalena's *la galera* exercised complex and inconsistent practices of *recogimiento*. In both institutions, exemplarity was predicated on the continued defiance of women. Analysis of these two institutions brings to the forefront the tensions between rehabilitative models and practices. The relationship between the goals and outcomes of institutional practices are not as clear-cut as proposals and institutional manuals indicate, and the outcomes of distinct institutional practices vary significantly among women.

The comparative nature of this project has allowed for the study of two separate phenomena and the connections between them: the actual penalization and containment of women (in the magdalen house and the *galera*) and the staging of rehabilitation and punishment in the *comedia*. The project encompasses theatrical texts, institutional manuals, personal correspondence, legal documents, and economic records, following Natalie Zemon Davis's directive to explore fiction alongside and within the archive (i.e., the text within its cultural context). Public theatre and early modern custodial institutions enjoyed an often fruitful interdependent social and economic relationship. Although moralists claimed that public theatre, especially the display of the actress's body, caused bad behaviour or illness, its popularity directly subsidized the creation and maintenance of custodial institutions. Theatre thus played a critical role in this long-standing spiritual and sexual economy, where the wages of sin were used to pay for the rehabilitation of women. We can and should examine issues of deviance, norms, and containment through various lenses that allow us to understand both the pressures placed on women to "contain" themselves sexually and morally as well as the multifaceted ways that the public stage allowed for an exploration of the implications, variations, and meanings of that moral economy.

While *Unruly Women* provides readers with a more complete introduction to the history and practice of custodial institutions for women, to date we have no detailed records (apart from names or numbers) that provide concrete details about the specific women who passed in and out of these spaces. The compelling images of unruly women on stage would certainly be complemented by the promise of fragmented biographies of these women, a task that can be accomplished through intensive archival investigation. The custodial institution took a variety of forms across the early modern period, encompassing the jail and magdalen house as well as, for example, orphanages, (syphilitic) hospitals, and homes for widows and abused wives. Similarly, significant work is still needed to contextualize the impact of these two institutions within the broad network of neighbouring institutions in Madrid, throughout Spain, and across the Atlantic. In the colonial context, repression of African, indigenous, and mixed-race populations in Spanish America produced a drastic increase in control of women and their sexuality; not surprisingly at the end of the seventeenth century, the number of female residents in non-penal institutions reached its peak. In Lima, for example, 20 per cent of women lived in church-sponsored sex-segregated institutions (Socolow 147–65). As Tamar Herzog sagely advises, "The colonial experience was instrumental to the understanding of Spain, and vice versa, in ways we have not yet sufficiently explored" (208).

As the previous chapters have shown, there are also a number of other plays that focus on rebellious women and their rehabilitation that merit additional study. Two notable examples that fall outside of the genre of the three-act *comedia* are the *entremés*, *Las Mozas de la Galera* (The Interlude of the Girls in Prison) (1663) and the one-act *La Baltasara* (The Baltasara) (1652). These theatrical pieces are distinctive because they explicitly dramatize the topic of women's rehabilitation with clear references to contemporary social concerns. The first features bawdy women inmates in a brief comic interlude and the second performs the religious conversion of the real-life actress referenced in the play's title. The presumed staging of both pieces evidences a popular familiarity and concern with these social topics.

Through an examination of the proposal and practices of custodial institutions for early modern Spanish women and fictional representations of women's deviance on stage, *Unruly Women* probes the boundaries of the anxieties about women's sexuality and behaviour by connecting the realities of custodial institutions with the exploration of women's deviance on the public stage. Rather than neatly providing explanations, the project opens up new considerations of women's deviance in the early modern reality and the early modern imaginary, making way for further investigation of archival sources.

Epilogue

"Bad Girls" of the Spanish *Comedia*

We regularly punish those who fail to do their gender right.

Judith Butler, *Gender Trouble* (178)

The deviant heroine of the Spanish *comedia* dramatizes a variety of relevant social and political concerns that surround the topic of rehabilitation in early modern Spain as a contradictory practice of containment and assistance for women. The figure of this "bad girl" – a contemporary label I use here intentionally and provocatively – also illuminates an assortment of issues that are relevant and pressing for readers today. The topic of "bad girls" on the Spanish stage raises a number of important questions about the relationships between spectacle, gender norms, and exemplarity.

On the final day of an upper-division undergraduate seminar dedicated to this topic, I asked each student to consider the major themes of the course and to generate his or her own short list of contemporary "bad girls." The exercise served at once as an entertaining culmination to the semester and as a provocative corollary to our in-class and online discussions. During class we compiled a list that included any woman who appeared multiple times. The range of the overlaps were both surprising and suggestive, featuring pop stars (Britney Spears, Lady Gaga, Beyoncé, Rihanna, Amy Winehouse, Christina Aguilera, Miley Cyrus, Madonna), politicians (Hilary Clinton, Michelle Obama, Sarah Palin, Nancy Pelosi), and an array of major and minor celebrities (Angelina Jolie, Kate Gosselin, Chelsea Handler, Nancy "Octomom" Suleman, Lindsay Lohan, Courtney Robertson [of *The Bachelor*], Tiny Fey, Paris Hilton, Oprah, Pamela Anderson, and Ellen DeGeneres).

While the list certainly reflects the particularities of my American private university classroom, it also demonstrates an array of characteristics that are compelling in the context of this project. Certainly it is possible to compare the rumours (real or alleged) that circulated around early modern Spanish actresses to the kind of celebrity gossip that surrounds contemporary pop stars, also critiqued for their overt displays of sexuality and their violation of set moral codes. When Britney Spears suffered a mental breakdown in 2007, the fact that she shaved off her head of hair became the most widely discussed evidence of her mental instability.[1] In 2011 Miley Cyrus received a Bob Marley cake for her birthday and gossip circulated that the actress had a problem with marijuana.[2] In his 2012 memoir about his daughter Amy Winehouse's battle with alcoholism, Mitch Winehouse blames her ex-husband Blake Fielder-Civil for her drug and alcohol addiction.[3] It is also worth exploring how and why these pop icons and their public and private conduct are often marketed to young women as exemplary. In these specific examples, public acts by celebrities that vary dramatically in seriousness – involving hairstyle, birthday cake, and the influence of a bad husband – are offered to a general audience as cautionary tales.

Likewise, it is suggestive to compare the representation of the female political figures from my students' lists to the early modern figure of the masculine woman as well as to displays of austere piety enacted by elite, royal women of the period. Their political voices (although wildly varied) are certainly bolstered or mediated by constructed displays of masculinity and femininity to construct or critique their own popular perception. For example, Ann C. McGinley argues that Hilary Rodham Clinton was an unpopular figure because she was the first First Lady to maintain her professional career and was perceived by some as not prioritizing her obligations as wife and mother. It was not until the Monica Lewinsky scandal that her popularity increased: "It was her feminine vulnerability that raised her popularity in the ratings" (717). Similarly Michelle Obama was critiqued for being too concerned with her appearance and having too muscular arms and was therefore too masculine.[4] Even the satirical publication *The Onion* made Obama's arms the subject of an article.[5]

The remaining array of celebrities named by my students offers another set of important characteristics for bad woman. These women encompassing a wide range of behaviours and are variously antagonized for their performances concerning their sexuality, mothering, drug and alcohol use, wealth, prominence, or even stand-up comedy.

Certainly playwrights of the early modern period would have crafted a masterfully entertaining three-act *comedia* that documented their notorious transgressions. The media already generated a character type when they named Nadya Suleman "Octomom" after the birth of her octuplets. The fact that she had six other young children and was unemployed contributed to existing anxieties surrounding assisted reproductive technology, social welfare programs, and Suleman's proclivity for reproduction. Another compelling example dialogues beautifully with María de Zayas's representation of female alliances. When the "bad girl" Courtney Robertson won the affection of *The Bachelor* in the 2012 series, other contestants on the show as well as fans were outraged that a woman so deceitful could have won the prize of marriage. In fact, in the 12 March 2012 "Woman tell all" reunion episode, Courtney was confronted and publicly chastised for her actions, described by the other contestants as a "black widow," "vindictive," "manipulative," "a liar," "hurtful," and "in it to win it." The episode ended with a tearful public apology from Robertson, and so the show projected the idea that the contestant had changed.

Though reality television is worlds away from early modern public theatre, the intrigue and mass popularity of the two formats for audiences is worth taking into serious consideration and comparison between the two genres proves a lively topic for energized classroom discussion. As a group, these contemporary "bad girls" largely serve to highlight the various ways in which women are stigmatized or punished because they defy gender norms, true for the early modern period as well as today. Or, in the words of my students, these women are perceived as "bad" because they violate set social norms, but it's really not their fault.

Conspicuously absent from this list is the woman as active criminal agent, "bad" because she chooses to be so. In recent years, cases such as those of Megan Ambuhl, Casey Anthony, Sabrina D. Harmon, Lynndie England, Susan Smith, Rosemary West, and Aileen Wuornos, unsettle standardized gender norms, implicitly challenging the very feminist concept of violence as masculine.[6] Barbara Ehrenreich, for example, expressed shock at the torture committed by US soldiers at Abu Ghraib, especially because women were involved as actors in the crime. She writes, "What we have learned from Abu Ghraib, once and for all, is that a uterus is not a substitute for a conscience" (2). Ehrenreich's statement echoes the predominant liberal feminist perspective on women and violence, which emphasizes the idea of women as victims of patriarchy, where women are passive and men are active. This view has enabled us to clearly examine the oppression of, and violence against, women. But this conceptualization of woman has its limitations. The idea of woman as a victim of violence and more broadly as a vulnerable subject renders paradoxical, if not impossible, the concept of the violent woman. If women are by nature caring, peaceful, and morally superior subjects, then the violent woman is the anomaly, manly, and maybe even not-a-woman. What does it mean to deny women the capacity to be "bad"?

In an attempt to answer this question in the context of global politics, Laura Sjoberg and Caron Gentry argue for the necessity of *seeing* bad women: "We, as scholars and political actors, must be willing to embrace and study the agency of not only the best of women but also the worst of women" (223). They argue persuasively that popular narratives in the mass media on women's acts of violence enforce gendered stereotypes and effectively limit women's freedom: "This is not to say that we dream of a world where all women are allowed to engage in suicide bombings and incite genocide ... however, idealized notions of femininity which trap (any) woman into an idealized role based on gender are a threat to, if not a reversal of, the 'rising tide' of gender equality" (222).

Women who commit violent acts should not be viewed as exceptional or unwomanly. Instead, new narratives on women in all their facets, including deviance, should be constructed, where passive femininity is not implicitly or inevitably better for women. By challenging the link between vulnerable women and femininity, it is possible to open the space in which powerful women can be observed enacting complex reactions to the circumstances they inhabit and inscribe. By compiling a body of evidence where defiant women both adhere to and resist social norms, it is possible to explore the ways in which punishment, penitence, and performance are intimately linked. Though these historical and theatrical characters are far removed from the context of contemporary experience, the comparison between the two periods is one practical way to create a sense of relevance for students, generating interest and enthusiasm for a time and place that can often appear difficult to access. It also creates a space to develop and utilize a critical eye that can be used to explore and contextualize the conflicting representations of gender, rehabilitation, and performance in early modern Spain as well as in their own world.

In the last year, the Magdalene House in Nashville, Tennessee, has been the subject of a three-part documentary on National Public Radio and the focus of a 2012 participant-observation account.[7] The Magdalene House is a two-year private, residential centre for women with criminal histories of prostitution and drug addiction, and is based on the spiritual principles of Benedictine rule. Founded in 1997 by Episcopal priest Becca Stevens, the home has graduated more than 150 women and has raised about $12 million in private funds. The women of Magdalene House range in age from twenty to fifty, and many have been sexually abused between the ages of seven and eleven, have been arrested on average a hundred times, or have spent about twelve years on the street as prostitutes.[8] To generate income for the Magdalene House and learn marketable skills, the residents make what Stevens calls "healing products," bath and body products and candles through their associated small business, Thistle Farms.[9]

The reformed model of rehabilitation for recovering prostitutes certainly reflects new ideas about ways to effectively support women who wish to leave their life on the streets. Placing the Magdalen House into a historical institutional context also makes apparent some of its common features with the magdalen house model of the early modern period, particularly the undertones of its religious and economic structure. The production of bath and body products has clear referents to Mary Magdalen's traditional association with curative or perfumed oils or ointments. Rehabilitative institutions directed specifically at female prostitutes is still a topic that generates considerable public attention, and so provides a means for contextualizing some of the ongoing and most meaningful social concerns the topic still generates, such as the regulation of prostitution and gender-specific practices of recovery.

By constructing a narrative of "bad girls" who both challenge and enforce the proscriptive attitudes and advice assigned to them by contemporaries, my hope is that students today will also become attentive to their own attitudes about the standards and rules that produce and dictate gendered behaviour, as well as to their own performances of contemporary proscriptive norms. Most important, I seek to foster a critical space in which it is possible to resist and redefine the systems of rehabilitation and punishment used to punish those who deviate from the norms assigned to their gender.

Appendix 1A

Reason and Form of the Galera and Royal House (1608)

MAGDALENA DE SAN JERÓNIMO[1]

To the King, Our Lord:

Having contemplated and seen, with many years of experience, what a large part (if not the largest) of the harm and havoc customary in this kingdom of Spain is born from the liberties, dissolution, and destructiveness of many women, I felt (although myself a great sinner) a deep pain in my soul, as to see our great King and Lord offended, just as to see this very noble and Christian kingdom lost and broken.

This suffering often times made me contemplate and search for some kind of remedy for such evil. I, among many others, volunteered myself for the cause. Although severe, I seemed the best and most efficient. After four years, I returned to the Court and proposed to Your Majesty the reasons upon which I based my claims. Your Majesty, with your usual benignancy and clemency, listened to me with time and attention, and judging the goals I represented to be worthwhile, sent me to speak with the Duke of Lerma and other advisors, so that they could put the project into effect, as they have done in this Court of Madrid and in Valladolid. Just like other new things at their start, this one has aroused novelty and admiration, not only among the vulgar and common people, but even among the best; and more serious, the name and acts of this *Galera* are considered too rigorous and severe, as it was invented by a woman against women. Although the approval of Your Majesty and all of your council and the rewards of the project in this short time was enough to satisfy everyone, with all of this I have wanted to write a small treatise in which I explained the importance and necessity of this *Galera* in order to provide complete satisfaction. Then, since this little work will appear in public, how could it be better received and more secure than under the shadow and protection of Your Majesty? How could this new *Galera* enter the sea to battle the various waves and storms of the stares and judgments of the vulgar without the steering wheel and rudder manned by such an apt captain as Your Majesty, who with your knowledge approved and with your power ordered the execution of this project. I beg Your Majesty to accept this small service and to bring forward this treatise, for much good and reformation of the kingdom and for the glory of our Lord, who guards Your Majesty through long and happy years in his holy service, just as we your servants need for you. Madrid, etc.

Magdalena de San Jerónimo.

Introduction

If man followed the daylight and reason that God our Lord provided him, the unearthly grace and inspired virtues which adorned his soul and body, he would easily flee evil and abhor sin, and with gentleness and delight he would embrace good and conduct himself in virtue. He would not need God to walk with him with whip in hand, treating him like a slave; originally he was a noble and loving son, and with pure love, he would chiefly serve and honour his commandments. But since he was tricked by the evil of the devil and lost his unearthliness and purity, and his daylight and reason was left thin and blackened, he began without hesitation to throw himself at any cost into the depths of evil. From here came the Lord our God to draw the sword of his divine justice and not only with threats of the eternal torments of the afterlife that would bridle him, but also by punishing him with many harsh whippings, since pain causes reason and fear causes justice. All nations and people were also born from this same story; although barbarous, with a common intent and almost natural agreement they have created bloody and rigorous laws to stop and punish the evil-doers and delinquents. From here jails, cages, and dungeons were formed; from here racks, whips, exiles, galleys, and executions, and other uncountable torments. And even these are not enough to exhaust and teach these sinners. And with much pain the good people have frequently witnessed in this Kingdom of Spain, in the same cities and town we have already mentioned, women, around twenty years old, with their liberties and disillusion, or shamelessness, who have lost their fear of God and justice and have wreaked havoc and laughed in the faces of men. Watching this breaks my heart, and I have often thought about the root of such evil and how to remedy it. From my experience, I have found that the cause was that there was not sufficient punishment in Spain for this line of bad women, and for this reason, that the remedy would be to have just as many kinds of punishments for them as there are for delinquent men, since many of these women profitably benefit from their evil and sins. One of these punishments, and very general, for these evil-doing men in Spain is to send them to a galley (*galera*) for two or more years as best fits their crime. So there should also be galleys of their own style in which to punish these evil-doing women, where their crimes can be suitably punished. For this reason, the point of this treatise is to create a house, in each city and place where there is a necessity, with the name of *Galera*, where justice is executed and vagrant women, thieves, witches, sorceresses, and other bad women are punished according to their crimes.

So that the form and appearance of how to create these *galeras* can be best understood, along with the importance and necessity of this project, I wanted to write this brief little treatise, and for the most clarity and distinction I have divided it into five main points.

> *The first. On the importance and necessity of this Galera.*
> *The second. On the form and appearance of it.*
> *The third. Notes for the justice and ministers of the Galera.*
> *The fourth. On the benefits caused by it.*
> *The fifth. An exhortation to the judges and governors of the republic.*

But before anything else is written, I take as fact that here we do not touch nor stain the good and honourable women, of which there are many in each city, town, and place. They are the honour of women, a mirror of honesty, and an example of all virtue. Instead we address the rotten and evil women that assault the honesty and virtue of good women with their dissolution and evil.

First Point

On the importance and necessity of this *Galera*

In order to, with greater clarity and ease, shed light on the importance of this *Galera* and the many and grave reasons that moved me to make it, it is necessary to put forth the great evils and ruin that this kind of woman has delivered to the republic for the last twenty years, so that by the gravity of the illness and disease it be made known the importance and necessity of the medicine and remedy.

And so I speak my first point, that there are many idle and vagrant young women, and among them some young ladies sixteen and under, that live off nothing but unsavoury deeds. To this end, once night has arrived, they leave their caves like fierce beasts on the hunt. They place themselves by those cantons, by streets and homes' doorways, inviting those miserable men who wander about carelessly and, these ladies themselves being lassos of Satan, fall and make others fall into the gravest of sins. They go through the houses of gentlemen, where there are pages and other serviceable youth, they go to the stables; and the men, emaciated, with the circumstance at hand, fall miserably; and they, having wasted the whole night, or most of it, *recógense*[2] with their ungainly earnings towards their inns and houses, and there they waste the day sleeping, eating, and idling away until the night returns.

From this kind of person, in addition to the grave affronts they commit against our Lord, arises a great ruin in the republic, that, because many of them are ruined themselves, inflicts and spreads a thousand sickening and contagious illnesses to the meagre men, that, without cavil or fear, join with them; and these, joining once more with other, or their very own, women, if they are married, pass on to them the very same scourge; and thus, one of these contaminated ones is enough to contaminate a great many people. And this truth is shown well, for our sins, in the Hospital of the Resurrection and the lot, where they take remedies and ointments; for every bed there are a thousand men, and there are not enough here nor in particular houses, where more difficult cases go off to.

There are many others that, being hearty and good and with strength to work or serve, beg for alms and wander from house to house where they give regular alms, and frequently many of them are adulterous, and carry with them the bad men to *recoger* alms, and although some of them have never given birth they carry with them two or three creatures to draw pity; and with this they take the alms from the real shameful poor and from those that because of real necessity cannot work; and because these slothful women in such a way find their sustenance, they want neither to work nor to serve.

There are others who take a home upon themselves, with jobs as seamstresses and collar openers, or who polish shoes, and stitch, or do other similar jobs, and under these colours their house is a store of offence to God; sometimes sinning on their own account and other times taking in women for the very same purpose.

There are many others who serve as pimps and third-persons, who, in addition to doing many unsavoury tasks in their homes, enter other homes, and more important yet, bring about great havoc and fault, not only to the maids, but also to the daughters and still to the ladies, a great affront to God, dishonour of a family, and the scandal of all the people.

It has also been seen by experience, and a great deal of pain to the righteous, that there are many women, especially of more advanced age, that keep in a barn two or three girls, who with the pretence of begging for alms go about to many places, where they commit many affronts to God, and at other times the very same women are taken and sold, arranging the operation, as sheep to the slaughter; from this barn are sustained these bad women and they ruin many girls, and some have been encountered for ten years or even fewer, ruined all the same.

It has not been nor is it less than that heard in hearsay, the evil and ravage that for the last twenty years has lain in the owners, maidens, and girls of service, because in addition to there being no one that wants to serve, given the desire to live the life of a tramp, the ones that do come to serve do so poorly and are so full of vices, because they are either adulterous or thieves or pimps, that much trouble is suffered because of them; and others, because they serve, ask for so many conditions, that it looks as if they come in to dictate rather than to serve. They say they should be given permission to leave one or two nights a week, they ask if there are children, if there are many staircases, if the washing is done at home, if the well is outside, if there is any pewter, and other similar things, which they do not want in said house. Previously, if a maiden or girl entered to serve in a certain house, she did not leave it except for marriage or burial; but now they barely linger for a month before moving on to another house.

And so, in order to wholly or partly remedy that which is among us, such great evil, perdition, and ravage as that which lies in the republic, it is suitable for us toapply an efficient remedy; and, for this, the main object is to tackle the ruin in their principles. And because of this, in all the cities and towns, where it is convenient, there should be homes or schools, where all orphaned girls are to be collected, so that there they will be taught virtue, Christianity, and policy, removing them from the danger of being lost, from song, and from dishonest dancing, and other such unsavoury inclinations and customs among which they were brought up, and making them exercise virtue and Christian doctrine, and learn labour, policy, and good upbringing, so that, in time, they may serve in *recogidas* and honest homes, where they may be remedied and put in place after a few years.

This remedy is of great importance, because it serves to preserve and prevent so many ills, but for those who now wander and are already lost, punishment and rigidity are necessary, and this is to be done in this new *Galera*, and this is the main intent and goal for which I now labour.

Conversely, what shall I say of those further evils and injuries that are not lesser, in my own eyes, but greater than those up to now referred to, that these miserable women who are enemies of God and contaminators of the republic generate within it? Well it is that, with their bad example and scandal they are an opportunity and a stumbling block to many an honest and honourable woman so that they too may stumble into such evils, or, at least, to see themselves among great temptations and the danger of falling into them. How many there dwell in each city and place that desire to be good, guard their honour, and serve their God! Those that labour towards this end are seen toiling away day and night, and in spite of that, they do not so much as wear an honest dress, nor earn enough to achieve sustenance. Conversely, they see these ruinous women, without soil or work, but strolling and idling about with such trappings and jewellery, and every day, going from party to party, performance to performance, orchard to orchard, and from pastime to pastime; and it seems to them that soil, sustenance, and dress are earned much more easily and enjoyably that way; and the devil, who never misses a turn, comes to enliven the temptation; and thus, many skinny ones give themselves up and leave labour and give themselves up to this vice. This is the cause why cities and towns are being swamped by these women, and why they are often the solicitors of men.

Experience teaches that the bidders of girls hold great liability in this misuse and that they tend to be the best pimps, because given that they hold a coin for every girl that they place with a master, and another from the master or mistress that takes the girl, they say to the girls themselves: "Stay this month in that house, while I find you a better one," and hence they bring them uneasy and restless from one place to another, and many times they have them in their own homes; and what's more, if some are beautiful and of good looks, hold them there, vagrant, and with many affronts to God which are committed in their homes. And this I know myself, because many of those that I have *recogido* have told me that they were lost as a result of these bad mothers, that could better be called stepmothers and placed to row their life away in this *Galera*.

Appendix 1B
Razón y forma de la galera y casa real (1608)

MAGDALENA DE SAN JERÓNIMO

Al Rey Nuestro Señor:
Habiendo yo considerado y visto, con la experiencia de largos años,
que gran parte (si no es la mayor) del daño y estrago que hay en las
costumbres en estos reinos de España, nacía de libertad, disolución y
rotura de muchas mujeres, sentía (aunque gran pecadora) un gran
dolor en mi alma, así de ver a nuestro gran Dios y Señor ofendido,
como de ver este nobilísimo y cristianísimo reino estrago y perdido.

Este sentimiento y dolor me hacía muchas veces pensar y buscar
algún medio que fuese remedio para tanto mal. Ofrecióseme uno entre
otros, que aunque riguroso me pareció el mejor y más eficaz. Venida
a la Corte, habrá cuatro años, propúsele a V. Majestad; y, juntamente,
las razones en qué me fundaba. V. Majestad, con su acostumbrada
benignidad y clemencia, me oyó de espacio y con atención, y juzgando
ser muy importante para el fin que yo pretendía, me mandó que lo
comunicase con el Duque de Lerma y con los del Consejo, y que con
efecto le pusiesen en ejecución, como se ha hecho en esta Corte de Madrid y en Valladolid. Como las demás cosas nuevas en sus principios,
así ésta ha causado novedad y admiración, no sólo en la gente vulgar
y común, pero aún en la principal; y más grave, teniendo el nombre
y hechos de esta *Galera* por demasiado rigor y severidad, particu-
larmente siendo inventada por mujer contra mujeres. Aunque para
satisfacer a todos bastaba la aprobación de V. Majestad y de los de
su Consejo, y el fruto que en este breve tiempo ya se echa de ver, con
todo eso he querido en un pequeño tratado escribir las razones de la
importancia y necesidad de esta *Galera,* con todo la demás que a ésta
pertenezca, para dar a todos entera satisfacción. Pues, habiendo de
salir en público esta obrecilla, ¿cómo podía salir mejor y más segura
que debajo de la sombra y protección de V. Majestad? ¿Cómo podía
entrar esta nueva *Galera* en la mar a contrastar las varias olas y vientos
de los varios pareceres y juicios del vulgo sin el timón y gobernalle de
tan sabio piloto como V. Majestad que con su saber la aprobó y con
su poder la mandó ejecutar? Suplico a V. Majestad se digne aceptar

este pequeño servicio, y llevar adelante esta obra, para mucho bien y reformación de estos reinos y gloria de nuestro Señor, el cual guarde a V. Majestad largos y felices años en su santo servicio, como todos sus vasallos habemos menester. Madrid, etc.

Magdalena de San Jerónimo

Introducción

Si el hombre siguiera la razón y luz natural de que Dios nuestro Señor le dotó, y la sobrenatural de la gracia y virtudes infusas con que adornó su alma y potencias, fácilmente huyera del mal y aborreciera el pecado, y con suavidad y deleite abrazara el bien y se ejercitara en toda virtud, no fuera menester que Dios anduviera con él como con esclavo en el azote en la mano; antes, como hijo noble y amoroso, por puro amor, le sirviera principalmente y guardara sus mandamientos. Pero como, engañado por la malicia del demonio, perdió lo supernatural y gratuito, y la razón y luz natural quedó flaca y oscurecida, comenzó sin freno ni rienda a arrojarse a toda suerte de vicios hasta despeñarse en el profundo de toda maldad. De aquí vino a que Dios nuestro Señor desenvainase la espada de su divina justicia, y no sólo con amenazas de los tormentos eternos de la otra vida le enfrenase, sino con muchos y graves azotes en ésta le castigase, porque siquiera por la pena fuese cuerdo, y por el temor hiciese virtud. De aquí también nació que todas las naciones y gentes, por bárbaras que sean, con un intento común y casi natural consentimiento hayan hecho leyes sangrientas y rigurosas para refrenar y castigar los malhechores y delincuentes. De aquí tuvieron principio las cárceles, bretes y calabozos; los grillos, esposas, cadenas y cepos; de aquí los potros, los azotes, destierros, galeras y muertes; y otros tormentos infinitos casi sin cuento. Los cuales aún no bastan para agotar los pecados y escarmentar los pecadores, como con harto dolor de los buenos se ve por los ojos en estos Reinos de España, señaladamente el algunas mujeres, que, de veinte años a esta parte poco más o menos, con su libertad y disolución, por no la llamar desvergüenza, han perdido el temor a Dios y la justicia, y hecho increíble riza y estrago en los hombres y en las mismas ciudades y pueblos, como adelantes diremos. El ver esto me quebraba el corazón, y pensaba muchas veces cuál sería la raíz de tanto mal y cuál el remedio de él. Dando y tomando hallé por mi cuenta que la causa era no haber bastante castigo en España para este linaje de malas mujeres, y que así, que el remedio sería que hubiese tantas suertes de castigos para ellas como hay para los hombres delincuentes, pues muchas de ellas les llevan harta ventaja en la maldad y pecados. Uno pues de los castigos, y muy general, que hay en España para los hombres malhechores es el echarlos a galeras por dos o más años según sus delitos lo merecen. Pues así haya galeras en su modo para echar a las mujeres malhechoras, donde a la medida de sus culpas sean castigadas. Por lo cual, el fin y blanco de esta obra es hacer una casa en cada ciudad y lugar, donde hubiere comodidad, con nombre de Galera, donde la justicia recoja y castigue, según sus delitos, las mujeres vagantes, ladronas, hechiceras, alcahuetas, y otras semejantes.

Para que se entienda la forma y traza como esto se ha de hacer, la importancia y necesidad que de ella había, con todo lo demás que a esto pertenece, quise escribir este breve Tratadillo, y para mayor distinción y claridad repartirle en cinco puntos principales.

El primero. De la importancia y necesidad de esta Galera.
El segundo. De la forma y traza de ella.
El tercero. Los avisos para la justicia y para los ministros de la Galera.
El cuarto. De los provechos que de ella se siguen.
El quinto. Una exhortación a los jueces y gobernadores de la república.

Pero antes de comenzar a decir nada, presupongo que aquí no se toca ni se pone mácula en las mujeres buenas y honradas, de las cuales hay muchas en cada ciudad, villa y lugar, que son honra de mujeres, espejo de honestidad y ejemplo de toda virtud, sino de las podridas y malas, que afrentan la honestidad y virtud de las buenas con su disolución y maldad.

Punto primero

De la importancia y necesidad de esta Galera

Para que con mayor claridad y facilidad se eche de ver la importancia de esta Galera y las muchas y graves razones que me movieron a hacerla, será necesario poner aquí los grandes males y daños que este género de mujeres hacía de veinte años acá en la república, para que por la gravedad de la enfermedad y dolencia se conozca la importancia y necesidad de la medicina y remedio.

Digo pues lo primero, que hay muchas mujeres mozas vagamundas y ociosas, y entre ellas algunas muchachas de dieciséis y menos años, que no se sustentan de otra cosa, sino de mal vivir. Para esto, llegada la noche, salen como bestias fieras de sus cuevas a buscar la caza. Pónense por esos cantones, por calles y portales de casas, convidando a los miserables hombres que van descuidados y, hechas lazos de Satanás, caen y hacen caer en gravísimos pecados. Vanse por las casas de los señores, donde hay pajes y otra gente moza de servicio, vanse hasta las caballerizas; y los hombres, flacos, teniendo a la mano la ocasión, caen miserablemente; y ellas, habiendo gastado toda la noche o la mayor parte de ella, recógense con su torpe ganancia a las posadas y casas que tienen, y allí gastan el día en dormir, comer y holgar hasta que vuelva la noche.

De este género de gente, además de las graves ofensas que se hacen contra nuestro Señor, se sigue un gran daño en la república, que, como muchas están dañadas, inficionan y pegan mil enfermedades asquerosas y contagiosas a los tristes hombres, que, sin reparar ni temer esto, se juntan con ellas; y éstos, juntándose con otras o con sus mujeres, si son casados, las pegan la misma lacra; y así, una de éstas contaminada basta para contaminar mucha gente. Y cuanta verdad sea esto lo muestran bien, por nuestros pecados, el Hospital de la Resurrección y los demás, donde se toman sudores y unciones, que para cada cama hay mil hombres; y no basta aquí ni en casas particulares, donde la gente de más pelo se va.

Hay otras muchas que, estando sanas y buenas y con fuerza para trabajar o servir, dan en pedir limosna y andarse de casa en casa a donde se dan limosnas ordinarias, y de ordinario muchas de ellas están amancebadas y llevan consigo los malos hombres para recoger la limosna, y aunque algunas nunca parieron van cargadas con dos o tres criaturas para mover a lástima; y con esto quitan la limosna a los verdaderos pobres vergonzantes y a los que por verdadera necesidad no puedan trabajar; y como estas tales mujeres holgazanas hallan de esta manera su sustento, no quieren trabajar ni servir.

Hay otras que toman una casita de por sí, con oficio de costureras y abrideras de cuellos, o que aderezan calzas, y toman puntos u otros semejantes oficios, y debajo de este color su casa es una tienda de ofensas de Dios; pecando unas veces por sus personas y otras acogiendo mujeres para lo mismo.

Hay otras muchas que sirven de alcahuetas y de terceras, que, demás de hacer en su casa mucho malos recaudos, entran en muchas casas, y aún principales, haciendo gran estrago y daño, no sólo en las criadas, pero aún en las hijas y aún en las señoras, con grande ofensa de Dios, deshonra de una familia y escándalo de todo el pueblo.

Hase visto también por experiencia, con gran dolor de los buenos, que hay muchas mujeres, especialmente de edad mayor, que tienen por granjería tener dos o tres muchachas, que con título de pedir limosna van a muchas partes, a donde hacen muchas ofensas de Dios, y otras veces las mismas mujeres las llevan y las venden, concertando el tanto más cuanto, como ovejas para el matadero, y de esta granjería se sustentan estas malas hembras y dañan muchas muchachas, y algunas se han topado de diez y aún de menos años estragadas del todo.

No ha sido ni es menor que los dichos, el mal y estrago que de los mismos veinte años a esta parte se halla en las dueñas, doncellas, y mozas de servicio, porque demás de no haber quien quiera servir, por andarse a la vida de gallofa, las que entran a servir sirven tan mal y están tan llenas de vicios, porque o están amancebadas o son ladronas o alcahuetas, que se padece con ellas mucho trabajo; y otras, ya que sirven, piden tantas condiciones, que más parece que entran para mandar que para servir. Dicen que se les ha de dar licencia para salir una o dos noches en la semana, preguntan si hay niños, si hay muchas escaleras, si se lava en casa, si está fuera el pozo, si hay peltre, y otras cosas semejantes, con las cuales no quieren estar en la tal casa. Antiguamente, si entraba alguna doncella o moza a servir en alguna casa, no salía de ella si no era para casarse o para la sepultura; pero ahora apenas duran un mes y luego mudan otra casa.

Pues para remediar en todo o en parte, cuanto en nosotros está, tan gran mal, perdición y estrago como hay en la república, conviene poner remedio eficaz; y, para esto, el más principal es atajar el daño en sus principios. Y por esta causa, en todas las ciudades y pueblos, donde haya comodidad para ello, se han de hacer casas o colegios, donde se recojan todas las niñas huérfanas, para que allí sean enseñadas en virtud, cristiandad y policía, quitándolas del peligro de perderse, de los cantares y bailes deshonestos, y otras muchas malas inclinaciones y costumbres en que se habían criado, y haciéndolas ejercitar en virtud y doctrina cristiana, y en aprender labor, policía y buena crianza, para que después, a su tiempo, puedan servir en casas recogidas y honestas, donde las puedan después de algunos años remediar y poner en estado.

Este remedio es de grande importancia, porque es para preservar y prevenir tantos males; pero para las que ahora andan vagando y están ya perdidas es necesario castigo y rigor, y esto se ha de hacer en esta nueva Galera, y es el principal intento y fin de que ahora yo trato.

Por otra parte, ¿qué diré de otro mal y daño no menor, a mi parecer, sino mayor que los hasta aquí referidos, que estas miserables mujeres enemigas de Dios y contaminadoras de la república hacen en ella? Y es, que con su mal ejemplo y escándalo son ocasión y estropiezo a muchas mujeres honestas y honradas para caer en semejantes maldades, o, a lo menos, a verse en gran tentación y peligro de caer. ¡Cuántas hay en cada ciudad y lugar que desean ser buenas, guardar su honra y servir a su Dios! Vense pues estas tales que para esto trabajan de día y de noche, y con todo eso no alcanzan para vestirse un vestido honesto, ni aún allega todo su trabajo para poderse sustentar. Por otra parte, ven que estas ruines mujeres, sin hacienda, sin trabajo, sino paseándose y holgándose andan muy llenas de galas y joyas; y cada día, de fiesta en fiesta, de comedia en comedia, de huerta en huerta, y de recreación en recreación; paréceles que se gana de aquella manera con más facilidad y más gusto la hacienda, el sustento y el vestido; y el demonio, que no pierde punto, acude a avivar la tentación; y así, muchas flacas se rinden y dejan la labor y se dan a este vicio. Lo cual es causa que estén las ciudades y pueblos cuajados de estas mujeres, y que ellas sean ya muchas veces las solicitadoras de los hombres.

La experiencia enseña que las ponedoras de mozas tienen gran culpa en este mal uso y que suelen ser las mejores alcahuetas, porque como tienen un real de cada moza que ponen con amo, y otro del amo o ama que lleva la moza, dicen a las mismas mozas: "Estáte este mes en esa casa, entretanto que te busco otra mejor," y con esta ocasión tráenlas inquietas y desasosegadas de una parte a otra, y muchas veces las tienen en su casa; y más, si algunas son hermosas y de buen parecer, tiénenselas allí vagantes y con muchas ofensas de Dios que se cometen en sus casas. Y esto sélo yo, porque muchas de las que he recogido me han dicho que se habían perdido por causa de estas malas madres, que mejor se podían llamar madrastras y echar a remar su vida en esta Galera.

Appendix 2A

Historical Compendium and Instructive Manifesto on the Origin and Foundation of the Royal House of St Mary Magdalene of the Penitence, commonly known as the Recogidas of Madrid

MANUEL RECIO (1777)

Chapter One: On the Origin and Foundation of the Royal House of St Mary Magdalene of the Penitence

The foundation of the Royal House of St Mary Magdalene of this Imperial and Crowned Town of Madrid (which is the most holy institution held by the Catholic zeal of our King) had its origins in 1601 in a home for travelling pilgrims. It was founded by the Confraternity of Vera-Cruz and Our Lady of Grace on the calle de los Peregrinos. Doña Ana Rodríguez donated a home to this cause, where it served as a Hospital under the watch of Octavio Centurion, Hermano mayor nominated by the confraternity.

This *retiro* or *recogimiento*, the Royal House of St Mary Magdalene, had its origins in 1618, as was stated in an *Auto* of 27 April 1619 with the consent of the Royal Advisors, the State Council, and Supreme Council of Castille, and its President, the Illustrious Señor Don. Fernando de Acevedo, Archbishop of Burgos.

[...]

As the holy mission of the house was designed to *recoger* these women, who had lived immorally and, touched by the powerful hand of God, had retired to this house to do penitence for their excesses which had led to their freedoms; they were given rules and prudent statutes, and, appropriate for this purpose, they attend also to the health, strength, and build of these women.

Chapter Two: Moving the *Recogimiento* to la calle de Hortaleza

In the year 1623 Señor Don Francisco de Contresras, President of Castille and Protector of the House, decreed that the *Recogimiento* on the
calle de los Peregrinos be moved elsewhere, because the House it occupied was very small. He also intended to sell the House in order to
help pay for the new foundation; yet the Confraternity of la Vera-Cruz,
as the owner that it was, argued against this in the Council, and won
executive powers in its favour.

So that the move of the Sisters be effective, as Señor Protector wanted
and required, a house was bought on the calle de Hortaleza that had
been owned by the chief officer; and once the corresponding work that
was destined for it was carried out, the Sisters' move was made in the
following manner:

They brought them in procession and passed them by the Monasterio de las Señoras Descalzas Reales, where the Kings waited to see
them; there they all sang a prayer while prostrating themselves on the
ground, an act that inspired much devotion. They went two by two,
dressed in a robe of fitted white, and a white wool cloth, or mask, cov-
ering their faces, and in this way they arrived to the new *Recogimiento*,
where they were received by the President.

Chapter Three: Building a New House, and Church

The year 1637 arrived, and the Sisters, finding their room a bit narrow
and very battered, went to H.M. to make known their necessity: That
the House they occupied was threatened by ruin and was in great risk
of sinking: That the number of *Arrepentidas* was increasing, and other
things they could not admit, because there was no place to put them.
And attending to their pleas, Señor D. Felipe IV served by calling the
Council to demolish the House, and labour anew; and the Council in
keeping with the Royal Resolution, lay down their Decree in the same
year of 1637, commanding the Village of Madrid to hastily give a financial advance of 80 ducats for the product, and value of the tax levied
on each quart of wine, for the construction of the Jail of the Court, and
charged this task, the one regarding the Casa de Ayuntamiento, and
the Village Jail (which were also made at that time) to the Licenciado
D. Josef Gonzalez, of H.M. Council and Chamber, and D. Antonio de
Contreras; and in effect the work of the House, and Church was done,

having bought for the creation of these a few things, that were had by Doña Ana Manzano, and Gabriel Arias together with the *Recogimiento*.

The Church, although small, is of very good architecture: the Image of Saint Mary Magdalene, which was placed in the last segment, over the architrave, and cornice of the altarpiece of the greater Altar, is a creation of D. Andres de los Elgueros.

Over the side door of the Church, at the side of the Epistle, there lies a great painting of Saint Mary Magdalene, a D. Juan Carreño original, of which D. Antonio Palomino makes great mention; in the front is another of St Joseph of the same size, a Wan de Pere original, although it is not of such merit; at both sides of the altarpiece of the greater Altar, over the doors of the sacristy and altar rail, there lie two beautiful paintings of two ovals, one of St Onofre, a Francisco Palacios original, whose head is mistaken for the best of the Españoleto, and the other is a St Francis, a Dominico Greco original, of the best time and taste of the Author's. There is also in the Church a painting of St John the Baptist, which is a copy of Hanibal, and another of St Gerónimo, which is a copy of Ticiano. In the Sacristy there is a small painting of St Joseph, an Alonso Cano original; and inside the House a few well-made copies of several and good Authors; and between them a painting of the Holy Christ of Burgos, a Mateo Zerezo original.

The Sisters live in this retreat with great *recogimiento*, in continuous exercise of prayer, penitence, and mortification, in the hopes that if in a past life they threatened the Republic, they may later help build it with their example.

Although in the first Constitutions, and Statutes, the best rules were given, and dispositions so that the institute be maintained with integrity, as time alters all things,when this House came under the protection of the Illustrious D. Juan de Layseca y Alvarado he found the saint wholly without use, as well as the laudable institute of its foundation. The Sisters that were admitted entered secretly by way of the porter's lodge, freeing themselves of the established one-time formality of one hundred ducats that they were to give to the House; the majority of those who entered were maidenly damsels of good manners, without method, or rules in their way of life, domestic governance, and obedience. It being necessary that those from a lowly lifestyle be together to serve God, they conformed themselves, and lived in observance, and common association, so that in that measure peace and union, which should be kept in the heart's interior, would manifest itself in the uniform guard of exterior habits. Under these terms, and to remedy this imperfection, and in order to prevent such successive prejudices, and the relaxations which spring from them, D. Juan de Layseca y Alvarado charged S.I. an ecclesiastic person, learned and of singular virtue, to arrange some Constitutions, to look in the best direction, and spiritual, and temporal government of the Home, so that these were guarded later, as precise rules, tending mainly to his institution.

And so they formed the Constitutions with such prudence, and success, that they deserved the approval of his Excellency Señor D. Antonio Ibañez de la Riva Herrera, Archbishop of Zaragoza, being the president of Castile, and the aforementioned Most Illustrious D. Juan Layseca.

The Sisters having in community found out about the new Constitutions, that were formed for their adherence, admitted them with much amusement, and they offered their fulfilment, and observance of these rules, and precepts, as they had practised since the year 1692.

In these famous Constitutions they are instructed on the model of their spiritual and temporal government, warning them of those things that happen most often in the ordinary life of seclusion.

In spite of the healthy maxims that these Constitutions contain, their precepts were altered with great prejudice towards the institute; by which the Lord Protectors Marquis of Andía, and D. Pasqual de Villacampa saw themselves forced to lay down their decrees, and providences, ordering their observance and fulfilment.

Appendix 2B

Compendio histórico, y manifiesto instructivo del origen, y fundación de la Real Casa de Santa María Magdalena de la Penitencia, vulgo las Recogidas de Madrid

MANUEL RECIO (1777)

Capítulo primero: Del origen, y fundación de la Real Casa de Santa María Magdalena de la Penitencia

La fundación de la Real Casa de Santa María Magdalena de esta Imperial, y Coronada Villa de Madrid (que es la obra del mas santo instituto que mantiene el celo católico del Rey) tuvo principio en el año de 1601 en la casa que para albergue, y recoger Peregrinos de noche, fundó la Cofradía de la Vera-Cruz, y nuestra Señora de Gracia en la calle de los Peregrinos; a cuyo fin destinó una casa, que la había cedido Doña Ana Rodríguez, y sirvió de Hospital cuyo gobierno estuvo á cargo de Octavio Centurion, como Hermano mayor que era de la nominada Cofradía.

De este retiro, ó recogimiento tuvo su origen el de dicha Real Casa de Santa María Magdalena, habiéndose formalizado su establecimiento en el año de 1618, como consta de un Auto, que en 27 de Abril del de 1619 acordaron los Señores del Real, y Supremo Consejo de Castilla, siendo su Presidente el Ilustrísimo Señor D. Fernando de Acevedo, Arzobispo de Burgos, y del Consejo de Estado.

[...]

Como el santo instituto de la Casa era dirigido a recoger en ella aquellas mujeres, que habían vivido licenciosamente, y que tocadas de la poderosa mano de Dios, se retiraban allí á hacer seria penitencia de los excesos a que las había conducido su libertad; se las dieron reglas, y estatutos muy prudentes, y apropiadas a este intento, atendiendo también en ellas a las fuerzas, salud, y complexión de las tales mujeres.

Capítulo segundo: Trasládase este Recogimiento á la calle de Hortaleza

En el año de 1623 dispuso el Señor D. Francisco de Contreras, Presidente de Castilla, y Protector de la Casa, se mudase el Recogimiento de la calle de los Peregrinos á otra parte, porque la Casa en que estaba era muy reducida. Pretendió también que esta Casa se vendiese para ayuda de los gastos de la nueva fundación; mas la Cofradía de la Vera-Cruz, como dueño que era de ella, lo contradijo en el Consejo, y ganó Ejecutoría en su favor.

Para que tuviese efecto la translación de las Hermanas, como quería el Señor Protector, y exigía la necesidad, se compró una casa, que en la calle de Hortaleza tenia el Condestable; y hecha en ella la obra correspondiente al fin para que se destinaba, se hizo la traslación de las Hermanas en la forma siguiente:

Lleváronlas en Procesión, y pasáronlas por el Monasterio de las Señoras Descalzas Reales, donde estaban los Reyes para verlas: allí cantaron todas una Salve, y al decir la Oración se postraron en tierra; cuyo acto causó mucha devoción. Iban de dos en dos, vestidas con un saco de sayal blanquecino ceñido y un paño blanco, ó antefaz por encima del rostro, y con este orden llegaron al nuevo Recogimiento, donde las recibió el Señor Presidente.

Capitulo tercero: Fabricase nueva Casa, é Iglesia

Llegó el año de 1637, y hallándose las Hermanas con estrechez en su habitación, y esta muy maltratada, ocurrieron á S. M. exponiendo su necesidad: Que la Casa que ocupaban amenazaba ruina, y estaba en gran riesgo de hundirse: Que le número de Arrepentidas se aumentaba, y no podían admitirse otras. Porque no había donde ponerlas. Y atendiendo á sus súplicas el Señor D. Felipe IV. Se sirvió mandar al Consejo dispusiese que se derribase la Casa, y labrase de nuevo; y el Consejo en cumplimiento de la Real Resolucion, expendió su Decreto en el mismo año de 1637, mandando á la Villa de Madrid aprontase 80 ducados del producto, y valor de la Sisa del maravedí que se había impuesto en cada azumbre de vino, para la fábrica de la Carcel de Corte, y encargó la Superintendencia de esta obra, la de la Casa de Ayuntamiento, y Carcel de la Villa (que se hicieron también en aquel tiempo) á los Señores Licenciado D. Josef Gonzalez, del Consejo y Cámara de S. M. y D. Antonio de Contreras; y en efecto se hizo la obra de la Casa, é Iglesia, habiéndose comprado para la fábrica de esta unas casas, que junto al Recogimiento tenían Doña Ana Manzano, y Gabriel Arias.

La Iglesia, aunque pequeña, es de muy arquitectura: la Imagen de Santa María Magdalena, que está colocada en el último cuerpo, sobre el arquitrabe, y cornisa del retablo del Altar mayor, es hechura de D. Andres de los Elgueros.

Sobre la puerta del costado de la Iglesia, á el lado de la Epístola, hay una gran pintura de Santa María Magdalena, original de D. Juan Carreño, de la qual hace particular mención, y elogio D. Antonio Palomino: en frente hay otra de igual tamaño de S. Josef, original de Wan de Pere, auqnue no es de tanto mérito: á los dos lados del retablo del Altar mayor, sobre las puertas de la Sacristía, y Comulgatorio, hay dos bellos quadros en dos óvalos, el uno es un S. Onofre, original de Francisco Palacios; cuya cabeza se equivoca con las mejores del Españoleto; y el otro es un S. Francisco, original de Dominico Greco, del mejor tiempo, y gusto de este Autor. Hay también en la Iglesia una pintura de S. Juan Bautista, que es copia de Anibal, y otra de S. Gerónimo, que es copia del Ticiano. En la Sacristía hay un pequeño quadro de S. Josef, original de Alonso Cano; y dentro de la Casa algunas copias bien hechas de varios, y buenos Autores; y entre ellas una pintura del Santo Christo de Burgos, original de Mateo Zerezo.

Viven las Hermanas en este retiro con grande recogimiento, en continuo exercicio de oracion, penitencia, y mortificacion, de suerte que si con la vida pasada escandalizaron la República, despues la edifican con su exemplo.

Sin embargo de que en las primeras Constituciones, y Estatutos se dieron las mejores reglas, y disposiciones para que se mantuviese el instituto con integridad; como el tiempo altera todas las cosas, habiendo entrado á la proteccion de esta Casa de Ilustrísimo Señor D. Juan Layseca y Alvarado, halló enteramente sin uso el santo, y loable instituto de su fundacion; pues las Hermanas que se admitían, entraban de secreto por la portería, dispensándolas las formalidades establecidas para la recepcion por cien ducados que daban por una vez á la Casa: la mayor parte de las que en ella entraban, eran doncellas recatadas, y de buenas costumbres: sin método, y reglas en su modo de vida, gobierno doméstico, y obediencia; siendo precisamente necesario que las que baxo de un modo de vida estaban juntas á servir á Dios, se conformasen, y viviesen en una observancia, é instituto comun, para que así la paz, y union, que deben conservarse en lo interior de corazon, se manifestase en la guarda uniforme de las exteriores costumbres. En estos términos,

y para remediar este daño, y evitar en la succesivo los perjuiciòs, y re-
laxaciones que de esto se seguia, encargó S. I. á una persona eclesiástica,
docta, y de singular virtud, dispusiese unas Constituciones, que mi-
rasen á la mejor dirección, y gobierno espiritual, y temporal de la Casa,
para que estas se guardasen en adelante, como reglas precisas, atendiendo principalmente á su institucion.

Formáronse las Constituciones con tanta prudencia, y acierto, que mer-
ecieron la aprobacion del Excelentísimo Señor D. Antonio Ibañez de la
Riva Herrera, Arzobispo de Zaragoza, siendo Presidente de Castilla, y
del expresado Ilustrísimo Señor D. Juan de Layseca.

Enteradas las Hermanas en comunidad de las nuevas Constituciones, que se habian formado para su observancia, las admitieron muy
gustosas, y ofrecieron el cumplimiento, y observancia de sus reglas, y
preceptos, como lo han practicado desde el año de 1692.

En estas famosas Constituciones se las instruye en el modo de su
gobierno espiritual, y temporal, precaviendo en ellas las cosas mas
menudas que pueden ocurrir en la vida común de la clausura.

No obstante las saludables máximas, que contienen estas Constituciones, llegaron á alterarse sus preceptos en grave prejuicio del instituto; por lo que se vieron precisados los Señores Protectores Marques
de Andía, y D. Pasqual de Villacampa, á expedir sus decretos, y provi-
dencias, encargando la observancia y cumplimiento de ellas.

Notes

Introduction

1 Cosme Pérez was arrested for sodomy in 1636 but later absolved from the charges, which led various critics including Sherry Velasco to speculate that he was also protected because of his celebrity status and dramatic ability (*Male Delivery* 120).

2 A custodial or social welfare institution is a generic term that refers to institutions designed to remediate persons often considered to be either sickly or defective members of society. For an introduction to the topic of custodial institutions for women, see Sherill Cohen's *The Evolution of Women's Asylums since 1500*, which focuses primarily on Italy.

3 Magdalen houses (also known as *casa de recogidas* in Spain) are convents that opened their doors to repentant prostitutes. They operated on the transformative potential of the figure of Mary Magdalene with the goal of converting prostitutes to either religious or married life and gained popularity during the Counter Reformation across southern Europe. See Lazar for a detailed study of the magdalen house and other religious reform projects in sixteenth-century Italy.

4 See, in particular, chapters 1 and 2 of Marsical's *Contradictory Subjects*.

5 I follow Lerner's call for a "woman-centered" history and Scott's recognition of gender as a "useful category of analysis."

6 "Moralists" as a general term refers to a variety of early modern Spanish scholars who were educated in the humanist tradition. They commonly wrote in conduct manuals on the proper education of individuals. For an introduction to this topic in a sixteenth-century context, see Ynduráin's *Humanismo y renacimiento en España* and Nauert's *Humanism and the Culture of Renaissance Europe*.

7 See Villalba Pérez (*Mujeres*) on female delinquency and urban spaces,
  Friedman on the legal status of early modern Spanish women, and Santo-
  Tomás on the relationship between city life and public theatre. Also see
  Sánchez Ortega for a concise and teachable overview of this period.

8 Varey and Davis's two-volume study is the first to catalog the economic
  connections between Madrid's public theatres and hospitals. An additional source of information on this topic is Cotarelo y Mori's *Bibliografía*, a
  monumental tome which considers not only the publication, presentation,
  and funding of various *comedias*, but also the advice and protests of its
  contemporary moralists.

9 There is also significant confusion between causes and treatments of social
  deviance and disease. Physical, economic, and circumstantial ailments
  were commonly treated as moral problems.

10 As Vollendorf explains, "For most women, the best chance for an education lay within the walls of those convents; the increase in foundations led
   to a marked rise in the numbers of educated women in Iberia" (*Lives of
   Women* 5).

11 The components of the rite included the *sambenito* of the condemned (the
   vesting of a penitential garment), the procession, the sermon, and the
   execution. The ceremony had to be announced to the public at least eight
   days in advance.

12 See also Brown and Elliott for an extended description of these events and
   their impact on court life and culture.

13 See for example Isabel Barbeito, Jodi Bilinkoff, María M. Carrión, Anne J.
   Cruz, Mary E. Giles, Elizabeth Lehfeldt, Barbara Mujica, Ángela Muñoz
   Fernández, Mary Elizabeth Perry, Allyson M. Poska, Nieves Romero-Díaz,
   Magdalena S. Sánchez, Stacey Schlau, Sherry Velasco, Lisa Vollendorf,
   and Barbara F. Weissberger, among many others.

14 Shergold and Varey's comprehensive volume offers 954 entries on actresses (1631–1703). Included in the study is the actress and author María
   de Heredia, another example of a historical figure directly connected with
   both public theatre and jails. According to Shergold and Varey, she spent
   time in prison for her illicit love life before becoming a writer. Her scandal-
   ous life was the object of satire by many contemporary authors, including
   Lope de Vega who referred to her as "Narcisa" (Narcissist) (Rennert, 375).
   She also figures as a prominent character in a well-known comic *Jácara*
   recounting the adventures of its protagonist "el Zurdillo." The actress
   appears in the following lines: "El Zurdillo de la Costa/ ya está muy acon-
   solado/ de ver a María de Heredia,/ en la galera remando" (The Zurdillo
   of the Coast/ is already so relieved/ to see María de Heredia/ rowing in
   the galley) (Pellicer 2:101–2).

15 John Jay Allen, Joseph Oehrlein, Hugo Rennert, José Ruano de la Haza, N.D. Shergold, and Teresa Ferrer Valls, among others, have made substantial contributions to the study of performance within early modern Spanish public playhouses.

16 Cotarelo y Mori (267); his monumental *Bibliografía* provides the most in-depth overview of this topic.

17 Unless otherwise indicated, all translations are mine.

18 Another example can be found in *Dictamen de Fray Agustín Dávila, electo de Santo Domingo y otros teólogos de Madrid sobre la permisión de comedias* of 1600, flagged by Dopico Black. It advises: "Que no representasen mujeres en ninguna manera, porque en actos tan *públicos* provoca notablemente una mujer desenvuelta, en quien todos tienen puestos los ojos" (Women should not perform in any way, because in such public acts everyone is provoked to look at the unveiled woman) ("Public Bodies" 86).

19 In her study of actresses' wills, Daniels also reports that most actresses only made enough money to survive, and many were in debt to tailors because of the significant costs associated with maintaining and altering their wardrobes (84).

20 The story also communicates an image of actresses as superficial, or even greedy. According to a 1627 letter catalogued by Joaquín de Entrambasaguas, Lope de Vega is said to have directly encouraged the Duke of Sessa to spoil his objects of desire with numerous tokens of affection, claiming that actresses best understand affection through the receipt of gifts (94–5).

21 Provisional details about these actresses and others can be found in the *Diccionario biográfico de actores del teatro clásico español* (2008), a digital archive coordinated by Teresa Ferrer Valls.

22 This anonymous, early seventeenth-century oil painting is currently housed in the Monastery of Las Descalzas Reales in Madrid (113 x 84 cms). It was first identified as a portrait of the actress by Elías Tormo in 1927 based on the similiarties between the actress and a later Eugenio de las Cuevas portairt of her son, Don Juan José de Austria (1629–79).

23 In her study on theatrical iconography, Alicia Álvarez Sellers discusses this painting in detail. Although she raises some doubts about the fact that it portrays La Calderona, she classifies the painting as "important theatrical evidence," particularly for its ability to demonstrate the popularity and accessibility of religious themes to a contemporary audience, the richness of the costuming, and the dramatic relationship between the two women, especially their gaze and gestures (294).

24 Archival records indicate that Baltasara de los Reyes (b. 1550s) was likely her stage name and she was celebrated on stage for her ability to perform male roles. Her legal name was Ana Martínez (Mérimée 214).

25 Key works on the presence of women in the prison system of early modern
    Spain include, among others, Almeda's *Mujeres y castigo*; Barbeito Car-
    neiro's *Cárceles y mujeres en el siglo XVII*, Dopico Black's "Public Bodies,"
    Pérez Baltasar's "El castigo del delito," Sherill Cohen's *The Evolution of
    Women's Asylums Since 1500*, Martínez Galindo's *Galerianas, corrigendas y
    presas*, Meijide Pardo's *La mujer de la orilla*, Yagüe Olmos's *Madres en prisión*,
    Ramón Laca's *Las viejas cárceles Madrileñas*, Perry's "With Brave Vigilance
    and a Hundred Eyes," Domínguez Ortiz's "La galera o cárcel de mujeres,"
    Vázquez González's *Las cárceles de Madrid*, Fernández Vargas and López-
    Cordón Cortezo's "Mujer y régimen jurídico," and Pike's *Penal Servitude
    in Early Modern Spain*. For work on Spain's magdalen houses, see Pérez
    Baltasar's *Mujeres marginadas*, Perry's *Gender and Disorder in Early Modern
    Seville* or "Magdalens and Jezebels in Counter Reformation Spain" (in
    Cruz and Perry, *Culture and Control*), and Sánchez Ortega's *Pecadoras de
    verano, arrepentidas de invierno*. For a complementary discussion of gender
    and social deviance in nineteenth-century Spain, see Tsuchiya's *Marginal
    Subjects*.
26 Madre Magdalena's galera was located only four blocks away from its
    predecessor, the Casa de Santa María Magdalena in Madrid.

1. Gendering *Recogimiento* in Early Modern Madrid

1 This elaborate scene of staging and audience is captured with great visual
   detail by the painter Francesco Rizzi (1614–85) in his *Auto de fe en la Plaza
   Mayor de Madrid* (Prado Museum, Madrid, Spain, 277 cm x 438 cm). The
   background of the painting features the royal family with high ranking
   court officials appearing on the balconies. On the left, Rizzi depicts a lavish
   carpet, an altar with a green cross, and the banner of the Holy Office. In
   the centre of the picture stand two inmates dressed in mitre and *sambenito*
   (penitential garment). On the right are the stands for the families of the
   accused and in the foreground are soldiers and donkeys.
2 The earliest writings on *Recogimiento* can be credited to Francisco de Osuna
   (1492?–1540?), Teresa de Ávila (1515–82), and Luis de Granada (1504–88).
   For comprehensive introductions to the topic of *recogimiento* in colonial
   Latin America, see Josefina Muriel, Nancy E. van Deusen, and Susan
   Socolow. See María Dolores Pérez Baltasar and Isabel Barbeito Carniero for
   a focus on early modern Spain.
3 *Recogimiento* as a positive spiritual practice is frequently discussed in
   conduct manuals and humanist treatises in the sixteenth and seventeenth

centuries. See, for example, the works of Pedro de Luján, Diego Pérez de Valdivia, Fray Luis de León, Cristóbal Acosta Africano, Juan de la Cerda, and Juan Luis Vives.

4 *Beaterios* were congregations of unordained women pursuing private religious devotions. See Perry's chapter, "Beatas and the Inquisition in Early Modern Seville," for a fascinating overview of their precarious social status (*Gender*). For an overview of the relationships between charity and gender in orphanages, see Sharon Strocchia, Nicolas Terpstra, and Valentina K. Tikoff. The early modern hospital had a much less defined function than it does today. Although its aim was broadly curative, it sought to heal physical, mental, and moral ailments, often poorly separated from one another. In Italy, for example, *Incurabili* hospitals often housed reformed prostitutes in the first half of the sixteenth century, especially in Venice and Genoa.

5 For an introduction to the relationship between early modern Spanish politics and cultural production, see Mariscal's aforementioned notion of "contradictory subjects" and Moreiras's "subjects in mourning," which underscore the impact of social expectations on the formation of individual identity. The principal idea is that personal identification and performance were heavily mediated by the expectations and requirements of competing social norms. These more recent critics supplement some of the traditional conceptions of the relationship between empire and culture set by Américo Castro, Norbert Elias, and José Antonio Maravall.

6 This is not to suggest that women did not find resourceful ways to combat these gendered economic realities. For example, Poska has demonstrated the ways rural women in Galicia made new kinds of community connections to support each other in the absence of husbands. Siena's analysis of records from St Thomas Hospital in London show that one out of every four women relied on other women to solicit funds for their admission for medical care.

7 As Ruth Pike makes clear, between 1592 and 1598 the Castilian Cortes repeatedly complained about the vagrant and licentious women who filled the streets of Spain (4).

8 Until 1978 in Spain, the crime of adultery was always attributed to women exclusively (Pérez Baltasar, "El castigo" 62). See also Francisco Tómas y Valiente for a useful overview of moral and legal restrictions placed on women's sexuality in early modern Spain.

9 See Pérez de Colosía Rodriguez ("La mujer" 59) and Meijide Pardo (151–66).

10 Lynn Brooks also accounts for abandoned or orphaned children who
   commonly found their ways into acting troupes and were frequently
   integrated into the families of actors, playwrights, and dancers (239). Perry
   explains how prostitution became a viable profession for many of these
   young girls (*Crime* 217).

11 Although Spain has been characterized for its steady economic decline
   across the sixteenth and seventeenth centuries, R.A. Stradling points to
   1627 as the peak of the economic crisis: "Beginning in 1627, serious harvest
   failures struck some of the kingdom's most fertile areas, and quickly developed into the most intense subsistence crisis for over thirty years. (By 1630,
   the towns of central Castile, including Madrid itself, were to be in the grip
   of starvation)" (69).

12 When Felipe II named Madrid the capital and home of the court, its population was between 20,000 and 30,000 people. At the end of Felipe II's reign
   in 1598, Madrid housed nearly 100,000 residents. By 1600, it was the most
   populated city in Spain; by 1630 it housed nearly 150,000 people (Ringrose
   197).

13 Madrid as the new capital can be read in terms of what Gary B. Cohen and
   Franz A.J. Szabo term the "embodiment of power" for new cities across
   Europe, where the influence of state and ecclesiastical institutions imprinted significant decisions in the design, architecture, and cultural life of
   these cities (2–3). See also J.H. Elliott's analysis of power and propaganda
   in relation to urban life and culture.

14 According to Jon Arrizabalaga, John Henderson, and Roger French, syphilis was always blamed on the "other," hence its many names: the French
   disease, Neapolitan pox, and so forth. It was recognized as a venereal
   disease from a very early stage in the epidemic. By the sixteenth century in
   Spain, Juan Ignacio Carmona García explains, the disease formed a common part of everyday life (210).

15 There were numerous magdalen houses in existence during this time
   throughout Spain and Italy.

16 Madre Magdalena's *galera* project can be read as a direct response to the
   treatise written by Cristóbal Pérez de Herrera, the reformer, physician
   and economist. In his *Del amparo y reformacion de los fingidos vagabundos*
   (1598), Pérez de Herrera proposed a centralized program of response to
   rising concerns about the problem of delinquency in Madrid, especially
   among "false beggars." While addressing the problem of the delinquent
   woman, he highlighted various spiritual and moral arguments concerning women's (uncontained) sexuality, as well as the economic and political costs of delinquency, crime, illness, and poverty to social order. In the
   treatise he petitioned Felipe III to create workhouses to punish and contain

women, and argued that existing custodial institutions did not adequately address these concerns. Like Madre Magdalena, he stressed the idea that current institutions contributed to the professionalization of criminals and throughout the proposal stressed the political urgency of the situation.

17 I have argued elsewhere that work on women's rehabilitation in early modern Spain, and especially Recio's manual, allows us to better contextualize the scenes of women's rehabilitation and deviance depicted in later *crónicas* ("Chonicling"). My contention is that the manual and its narrative of history are inflected with the author's contemporary preoccupations about the function of rehabilitative institutions for women.

18 Pérez Baltasar originally cites Quintana's *Grandezas de Madrid* (Capit. LXXXVII). It is somewhat difficult to explain why nuns left their convent to move into the magdalen house, although we might speculate that the move was motivated by lack of economic resources or shifting institutional or religious purposes.

19 In her book *Lesbians in Early Modern Spain*, Velasco attributes the strict control of women's relations within prisons to the anxieties (real and imagined) surrounding same-sex relations. She points out, for example, a report written by Cristóbal de Chaves on the jails in Seville, *Relación de las cosas de la cárcel de Sevilla y su trato*:

> Not only do the women talk like the male criminals but according to Chaves they also imitate their sexual activities by using an artificial penis or "strap-on" dildo: And there are many women who want to be more like men than Nature intended. Many women have been punished in the prison for making themselves into "roosters" with an instrument made into the shape of a penis, which they tied to themselves with straps. Such women are punished with 200 lashes. (Chaves 25–6, quoted in Velasco)

20 See Dopico Black's analysis of the intersection between Madre Magdalena's public works and her penchant for the collection of relics ("Public Bodies"). See also Barbeito Carneiro's impressive overview of the ways women's relics were circulated throughout the early modern period, "Reliquias en textos y contextos femeninos."

21 Barbeito Carneiro explains that Mariana de San José was chosen to run the Royal Monastery of the Incarnation because Margarita de Austria (wife of Felipe III) identified her as an expert in relics. Since its origin in 1616, "el relicario constituye la pieza más importante del Convento y una de las lipsanotecas más singulares dentro de las Fundaciones Reales españolas" (the reliquary is the most important part of the convent and one of

the most unique *lipsanotecas* within the Spanish royal foundations) (215).
Among the many relics guarded in the Royal Monastery of the Incarnation
is the body of Madre Magdalena's friend, Luisa de Carvajal y Mendoza
(1566–1614).

22 The exact date of the establishment of the *galera* in Madrid is unclear. On
the one hand, Pike explains, "Pérez de Herrera mentions it by name in
his *Relación de sus muchos y particulares servicios* (1618), but there are no
references to it in extant official sources until 1622" (5). On the other hand,
Gema Martínez Galindo writes, "la Galera de Madrid ya existiá en el año
1608 cuando Magdalena de San Gerónimo escribe su 'Obrecilla,' pues
alude a ella, y así lo confirman diversos documentos de la época"
(Madrid's *Galera* already existed in 1608 when Magdalena de San
Gerónimo writes her "little work," since she alludes to it and various
documents of that time also confirm this) (62).

23 All citations from Madre Magdalena's proposal come from Isabel Barbeito
Carniero's 2000 transcription in *Cárceles y Mujeres en el Siglo XVII*.

24 The most extensive critical work about these two women is contained
in Barbeito Carniero's study of relics. Further, Lisa Vollendorf has also
examined Carvajal's status as woman writer (*Lives* 57–73), Anne Cruz has
focused on her letters ("Willing Desire"), Elizabeth Rhodes has edited and
translated a series of Carvajal's letters (*This Tight Embrace*), and Magdalena S. Sánchez has focused on her role as female sovereign ("Sword and
Whimple"). It is worth contextualizing their correspondence within the
existing work of other prominent religious women writing letters during
the same period, including, for example, Madre María de Jesús Agreda,
María de Guevara, and Teresa de la Valle y Cerda.

25 Additional attention needs to be paid to the composition and genre of the
proposal as a literary and historical artefact. Consider the similarities and
differences between the genres of Recio's institutional manual and Madre
Magdalena's proposal. Both ostensibly offer institutional histories, while
at the same time are affected by the distinct demands of their audience
and economic motivations. Richard Kagan's 2009 study *Clio and the Crown*
differentiates between what he calls "ordinary" and "official" histories and
stresses the usefulness of this second category. While it can be tempting to
gloss over these "official" histories as simple propaganda, Kagan instead
describes these works as engaging in "what is colloquially known as 'spin,'
selective but still accurate readings of the evidence relating to a particular
happening or event" (5).

26 For example, she writes, "¿Cómo podía entrar esta nueva *Galera* en la mar
a contrastar las varias olas y vientos de los varios pareceres y juicios del

vulgo sin el timón y gobernalle de tan sabio piloto como V. Majestad que con su saber la aprobó y con su poder la mandó ejecutar?" (How could this new *galera* enter the sea to battle the various waves and winds of the many opinions and judgments of the vulgar without the steering wheel and rudder of so wise a captain as Your Majesty, who with your knowledge approved this project and with your power ordered its execution?) (San Jerónimo 66).

27 These sentences were nearly identical to those received by male convicts in jails.

28 Many custodial institutions of the period used workhouses for the production of cotton textiles.

29 The concern with the false beggar reflects a common concern across Europe with the figure of the trickster. See Natalie Zemon Davis (*Trickster*) or Anthony Grafton for excellent studies on this topic.

30 Katherine Dauge-Roth explains that during the period, criminals were commonly marked with symbols or abbreviated monograms that represented various punitive institutions. For example, "GAL" would be common shorthand for galley. After 1724, letters corresponded to specific crimes or sentences throughout much of Europe (127).

31 The painting (228 cm x 180 cm) is currently housed in Madrid in the Museo de la Real Academia de Bellas Artes de San Fernando.

32 See the appendixes for longer representative excerpts from the institutional manual and proposal of both institutions, both selected from the early chapters of the documents to highlight overarching organizational structures and goals. I include the excerpts in Spanish and in English translation in order to provide a larger audience of readers an extended opportunity to compare the rhetoric of the two institutional documents in an unmediated format.

2. Stage Widow

1 Pedro Calderón de la Barca (1600–81) wrote between 110 and 180 plays in his lifetime and was known as the unofficial director of dramaturgical activities for Felipe IV. As Donald Beecher notes, the earliest performance of *La dama duende* may be 4 November 1629, the *fiesta* for the baptism of Prince Baltasar Carlos, an event that takes place at the start of the play (12).

2 Jonathan Thacker writes that the play continued to be a favourite among Spanish audiences throughout the eighteenth century. It was also the first of Calderón's works to be staged outside of Spain (109).

3 Gabriela Carrión's 2011 monograph offers an extended meditation on the significance of the marriage plot for Ángela and other heroines of the *comedia*.

4 As Margaret Greer explains, "In 1627–28, just before the presumed 1629 composition date of *La dama duende*, there had been a sudden deterioration of the Castilian economy. Due to a variety of factors, including a large-scale minting of the copper *vellón*, the country was suffering from a severe rise in prices in that currency. After price-fixing and then withdrawing *vellón* coins in circulation, the crown in August 1628 devalued the *vellón* by 50 percent, bringing instant relief to the royal treasury but heavy losses to private individuals" ("The Self" 98).

5 All quotations are from the text by Calderón de la Barca. All translations of this play come from Donald Beecher and James Nelson Novoa's 2002 edition of *The Phantom Lady*. The prose reflects the translators' intention to capture "more spontaneous and colloquial registers" (58).

6 De Backer's monograph offers in-depth analysis of the numerous ways sixteenth-century widows of Toledo were able to bolster their own images through their roles as patrons, especially through the sponsorship of convents and funerary devotions.

7 William R. Blue, Margaret Greer, and Bárbara Mujica have observed this complication in their studies of the play.

8 For additional resources on the topic of widows in the early modern period, also see the introduction to Mirrer, *Upon my Husband's Death* (1–17) and Levy, *Widowhood and Visual Culture in Early Modern Europe*.

9 Don Luis, Ángela's brother, is continually preoccupied with maintaining the security of Ángela's room. Not surprisingly, he is wary when Don Manuel is invited to stay as a guest in their home, and comments that Ángela's room is so dark and secluded that even the sun hardly recognizes her presence: "Lo que más me siento es que sea / mi hermano tan poco atento, / que llevara a casa quiera / un hombre, mozo, teniendo, / Rodrigo una hermana en ella, / viuda y moza, y como sabes, / tan de secreto, que apenas sabe el sol que vive en casa; / porque, Beatriz, por ser deuda, / solamente la visita" (It's his cavalier insouciance that makes me so angry. Just look what he does, Rodrigo: he brings this young blade under our roof, knowing my sister is there – young, a recent widow, and so hidden away that even the sun can't find her out. Beatriz is the only one who can visit her and that's because she's a relative) (320–30).

10 J.M. Ruano de la Haza has commented that the cabinet can be read as an emblem of female honour or a divider between gendered spaces. María Martino Crocetti has read the *alacena* as a metaphor for women-controlled hymeneal space (see especially 52–3).

11 Ángela's performances as the Phantom Lady are also likened to the devil. Cosme for example, explains that letter-writing is the devil's art, underscoring the fear associated with this linguistic power. Likewise, both Manuel and Cosme frequently confuse woman with the devil, clearly reflecting misogynist beliefs of the time. Manuel, for example, states: "Si demonio, por demonio, / y si mujer, por mujer, / que a mi esfuerzo no le da / que recelar ni temer / tu amenaza, cuando fueras / demonio, aunque yo bien sé / que teniendo cuerpo tú, / demonio no puede ser, / sino mujer" (If you're a devil, speak as you are, and if you're a woman, then speak as one. You won't see me cringe or cower at any of your threats even if you are a devil. Yet I know that in having a body, you're not phantom but a woman) (1029–37). Or in Cosme's words, "Que es mujer diablo. / Pues que novedad no es, / pues la mujer es demonio / todo el año, que una vez / por desquitarse de tantas / sea el demonio mujer" (No question she's a devil. Women are like that the whole year through. So where's the surprise if the devil should decide to be a woman for a change to get his own back on them?) (1135–40).

12 In a later section of the monologue, Ángela likens her jewellery and dress to objects of betrayal: "él, a la luz escasa/ con que la luna mansamente abrasa, / vio brillar los adornos de mi pecho, / (no es la primer traición que nos ha hecho) / y escuchó de las ropas el ruido, / (no es la primera que nos han vendido); / pensó que era su dama" (in the pale moonlight he caught a glimpse of my jewels and heard the rustle of my skirt – nor am I the first woman to have been so betrayed. He took me for his beloved) (711–17).

3. Dramatizing Women's Community

1 The other four major dramatists are Angela de Azevedo (1600–?), Ana Caro Mallén de Soto (1600s), Leonor de la Cueva y Silva (1600s), and Feliciana Enríquez de Guzmán (b. 1500s). Zayas was born in 1590 in San Sebastián, daughter of Fernando de Zayas y Sotomayor and María de Barasa. Her father was an infantry captain who served as administrator for the 7th Count of Lemos and was awarded knighthood in the military-religious Order of Santiago in 1628 (Greer, *María de Zayas* 16). Because of her family's connections, as well as detailed references to other cities in her works, it has been suggested that Zayas may have travelled outside of Madrid, where she spent the greater part of her life. Zayas participated in one or more of the literary academies that flourished in Madrid, although it is also likely that she did not receive a formal education and instead taught herself to read and write (Olivares and Boyce 209). Between 1621 and 1639 she published

verses as part of prefaces to other works. Additionally, she published elegies to mark the deaths of Lope de Vega and Pérez de Montalbán, who both praised her work during their lifetime; Montalbán, for example, called her "the tenth muse." In 1637, Zayas published the first set of her celebrated *novelas, Novelas amorosas y ejemplares*. Ten years later, the second half, *Desengaños amorosos*, was published. These *novelas* reveal a series of stories about women deceived, often violently, by men, and it is for these works that Zayas is most famous. During the first half of the seventeenth century Zayas was the most successful female author in Spain; as Brownlee reminds us, only Cervantes, Quevedo, and Alemán surpassed her book sales (*The Cultural* 6). For excellent studies of Zayas's life and work, see Brownlee, Greer, and Vollendorf, as well as Yolanda Gamboa.

2 It is still unclear whether or not Zayas's play was ever performed in public during her liftetime.

3 For a concise introduction to the topic of staging the *comedia*, see N.D. Shergold's overview of Madrid's commercial theatre between the years 1604 and 1635 (209–36).

4 In this context it is suggestive to consider how both parts of Zayas's *novelas* are tied together by the narrative frame of a *sarao* (soiree) organized within the works by Lisis for an exclusively female audience. Soirees in the homes of the elite were common modes of distribution of literary and performance arts throughout the early modern period. Susan Paun de García believes that a soiree is likely the context in which Zayas's extant play was distributed, although it may have also been staged (40). When considering the topic of Zayas's play performed in a public forum, it is useful to consider Mercedes Maroto Camino's comments that "theatrical representation ... was the most public expression available at this time and was therefore considered the least suitable vehicle by means of which a woman might convey her ideas. Furthermore, publicity and publication became, when applied to women, synonymous with prostitution" (10).

5 Critical editions of Zayas's play and *novelas* were not published until the mid-1990s as part of a boom dedicated to early modern women's writing. Major anthologies published during this time included Olivares and Boyce's *Tras el espejo la musa escribe*, Kaminsky's *Water Lilies*, Mujica's *Sophia's Daughters*, and Soufas's *Women's Acts*. During this period, there were also a number of publications dedicated to women's monastic writing, including Merrim's *Early Modern Women's Writing and Sor Juana Inés de la Cruz* and Arenal and Schlau's *Untold Sisters*.

6 Robert Bayliss has observed the incongruity between current critical interpretations of Zayas's play, paying particular attention to the limitations

of an exclusively feminist approach. This chapter is indebted to Bayliss's observation that this critical incongruity has radical implications for the study of gender: "Fenisa destabilizes the cultural binary constructed around gender, a notion that resonates well with feminist critical theory; but if we are conscious of her role as the play's antagonist and anti-example, we are aware that it is precisely that defiance of the limits imposed upon her gender that gets Fenisa into so much trouble" (11).

7 Rereading friendship in early modern Europe is not a novel proposition; however, the majority of critical attention to this topic has focused on the role of male homosocial bonds and relations. In the early modern Spanish context see, for example, Sidney Donnell, Antonio Feros, and José Reinaldo Cartagena Calderón.

8 Magdalena S. Sánchez revises the longstanding view of early modern Spanish women as isolated subjects. Through close study of Empress María, Margaret of Austria, and Margaret of the Cross, Sánchez argues that women were able to form and negotiate crucial political and social networks. For an introduction to this matter in a broader European context, also see Stephanie Merrim, Susan Frye and Karen Robertson, Laura Gowing, Michael Hunter, and Miri Rubin (Hunter and Rubin are with Gowing in a co-edited volume), among others.

9 See Biblioteca Nacional, ms. 2577.

10 Despite their long-standing relationship, when Marcia presents Fenisa with a portrait of her lover Liseo, Fenisa instantly falls in love with him and betrays her friendship to Marcia. When Liseo later learns of Fenisa's affection, he begins to juggle relationships with the two women. Another skeleton in Liseo's closet is Laura, a woman he promised to marry but then abandoned. Although Fenisa prefers Liseo to her other men, she manages to maintain romantic relationships with both Juan and Gerardo, in addition to others.

11 All translations of Zayas's play come from Catherine Larson's 1999 narrative translation, *Friendship Betrayed*.

12 To more fully appreciate the particular demand of transparency and desirability exerted on the early modern wife, it is helpful to think again about the way adultery was defined during this period as exclusively the fault of the woman, even if she had no part in an extramarital affair. See chapter 2 for a lengthier discussion of this topic.

13 To best contextualize conceptions of love in the early modern period, see Alexander A. Parker. Through a thorough analysis of canonical fifteenth-, sixteenth-, and seventeenth-century texts, Parker offers a comprehensive overview of the way love has been traditionally represented by literature of the period.

14 Joseph reads against this "romance of community," highlighting the works of Cherríe Moraga, Gloría Anzaldúa, Audre Lorde, and bell hooks, among others, for their critique of "singular identity categories as an organizing principle for social change. These works make it clear that to imagine women are a community is to elide and repress differences among women, to enact racism and heterosexism within a women's movement that is so marked by a particular (bourgeois) class position that it cannot address the concerns of "other' women" (xxii). In Joseph's view community is a dangerous category because it fails to recognize differences among women.

4. Women's Exemplary Violence

1 Luis Vélez de Guevara (1578–1644) wrote *La serrana de la Vera* during a trip to Valladolid. The manuscript of the play is preserved in the Biblioteca Nacional de Madrid and was transcribed and studied in 1916 by Ramón Menéndez Pidal and María Goyri de Menéndez Pidal. Vélez de Guevara was a prolific poet and playwright, having completed nearly 400 plays between 1600 and 1644 in addition to his satirical novel *El diablo cojuelo* (The Crippled Devil) (1641). For a more comprehensive introduction to his life and work, see Cotarelo y Mori's *Luis Vélez de Guevara y sus obras dramáticas*, Kennedy's *Studies in Tirso,* Vol. 1, and Hauer's *Luis Velez de Guevara.*
2 By the seventeenth century, the particular figure of the *serrana* is staged by a number of playwrights including Lope de Vega, Tirso de Molina, and Valdivielso with depictions certainly influenced by their literary foremothers: The Chata from the *Libro de Buen Amor* and the monstrous mountain woman of pastoral poetry. Laskier Martín explains:

> Most critics who have studied medieval *seranillas* believe that, for the most part, the poems are derived from the Provenzal *pastourelle*. This class of courtly lyric describes the encounter between a gentleman and a peasant girl or shepherdess whom he seduces, deceives, or rapes in order to satisfy his base and immediate needs … in Spain, the shepherdess becomes a *serrana*, the mountain woman native to the Iberian Peninsula who not only can be less refined, shy, and deliciate than the Provenzal *bergére* but can even be grotesque. Because of her lack of refinement, the *serrana* has been identified with the monstrous women of the medieval tradition. (152)

For a broader discussion of the mountain woman and her impact on the literature and culture of medieval and Renaissance Spain, see Marina Brownlee and María Eugenia Lacarra. Although the concept of the mountain woman is at least part source of the masculine woman character type,

I follow Matthew Stroud's lead as he describes Gila as "the *mujer varonil* par excellence" (*Plot Twists* 123). For a comprehensive introduction to the topic of the masculine woman character type in Spain, see McKendrick's *Woman and Society*.

3 Many critical approaches to the play have helpfully emphasized how its combined mythological, popular, and pastoral elements qualify it as a product of multiple genres, borrowing from what Góngora named the two classes of *serranas*: the mythological (Diana) and the oral *romancero* (Santillana or Arcipreste de Hita) (Enrique Rodríguez Cepeda 17). Cepeda is the editor for the edition of *La serrana* I use.

4 The actress is also commonly referred to by the name Josefa Vaca in various archival documents.

5 *La serrana de la Vera* has not been previously translated. In this chapter I offer initial narrative translations for the play.

6 José Sánchez Arjona also cites extramarital relationships with the Dukes of Pastrana, Feria, Rioseco, and the Marquis of Alcañices, Villaflor, and de Peñafiel (118–20).

7 The topic of Vélez de Guevara as tragedian generated a very interesting debate between Whitby, "Some Thoughts on Vélez as a Tragedian," and Parr, "Some Remarks on Tragedy and on Vélez as a Tragedian: A Response to Professor Whitby." Each author traces how Vélez de Guevara reworks the classic tragedy formula in his baroque context, for example, and highlights the ways protagonists uniquely possess a *hamartia*, or tragic flaw. The articles speak to the difficulty of the genre and caution against monolithic readings of the author that would reduce his tragedy to a simple formula.

8 Ruth Lundelius has attributed this combination, what she calls "the opposite of antitheses," to Vélez de Guevara's baroque style. She emphasizes Gila's juxtaposition of masculine and feminine, aggression and passivity, strength and beauty, which culminates in "an ever augmenting realization of just how bizarre a social misfit she really is" (230).

9 In her analysis of Queen Isabel in various Spanish *comedias*, María Y. Caba aptly remarks that the presence of the Catholic queen offers the audience a privileged perspective from which to analyse the interrelationship between politics, social structure, and gender in seventeenth-century Spain (132).

10 The motto *Tanto monta* is inscribed on the shield of the Catholic Monarchs, which placed the Isabelline arms of Castile and León in the upper-left quadrant, over the arms of Aragon. The royal design and motto appeared on royal seals and were widely incorporated into both public and domestic spaces. As Barbara Weissberger explains, "The importance of that ordering is shown by

the fact that it was the very first stipulation of the *Acuerdo para la gobernación del reino* (better known as the *Concordia de Segovia*) that Isabel and Fernando signed in January of 1475, just weeks after her accession to the throne. The agreement required that Isabel's arms precede Fernando's on all chancery documents; the inverse order was stipulated for their signatures" ("Tanto" 44).

11 Iván Cañadas reads this scene as a condemnation of Don Lucas. In his view, the problem with the match is the "crime of status, a crime which leaves the doubly marginalized peasant woman with no adequate means of address" (48).

12 The scene can be analysed in terms of *esturpo*, a concept Renato Barahona claims to determine "key facets of courtship, seduction and abandonment" for sex crimes in sixteenth- and seventeenth-century Vizcaya (7).

13 The stage directions here are most interesting, as they emphasize the sensuous yet statue-like qualities of Gila newly transformed into the *serrana*: "GILA la serrana como la pinta el romanze, sin hablar" (The *serrana Gila* as she is portrayed by the romance, without speaking) (57). See Brownlee for a parallel discussion of the *serrana's* "invasion" into the *Libro de buen amor* ("Permutations" 98–101).

14 Although Christopher D. Gascón does not include Gila in his study of female religious figures in early modern *comedias*, his theoretical framework is provocative in the context of this scene, particularly the idea that religious heroines visibly struggle on stage with their own identity, rendered by dramatists as "fluid and subject to change" (23).

15 Rambuss has paid special attention to the way desire seems to be produced by the penetration of arrows into the body of St Sebastian. See *Closet Devotions* (100–1).

Epilogue: "Bad Girls" of the Spanish Comedia

1 Denise Winterman, "Mark of a Woman." *BBC News.* http://news.bbc.co.uk/2/hi/uk_news/magazine/6375683.stm.

2 Jeannine Stein, "Miley Cyrus Quips about Marijuana." *Los Angeles Times.* http://articles.latimes.com/2011/nov/28/news/la-heb-miley-cyrus-marijuana-health-20111128.

3 Nick Watt, and Laura Effron. "Amy Winehouse's Father Opens Up." *ABC News.* http://abcnews.go.com/Entertainment/amy-winehouses-father-blames-singers-decline/story?id=16631194#.T-smxL_ymbQ.

4 Jeannine Stein, "Michelle Obama's toned arms are debated." *The Los Angeles Times.* http://www.latimes.com/features/image/la-ig-arms29-2009mar29,0,4782966.story.

5 "Michelle Obama's arms meet with Sri Lankan Refugees." *The Onion*. http://www.theonion.com/articles/michelle-obamas-arms-meet-with-sri-lankan-refugees,2743.

6 Ambuhl, Harmon, and England were three of eleven US military personnel convicted in 2005 for torture and prisoner abuse at Abu Ghraib prison in Baghdad. Anthony was indicted on charges of first-degree murder of her daughter. Although she was found not guilty of murder in 2011, the trial raised a number of questions about expected behaviours of mothers (fixed ideas about the displays and expressions of grief and an investment in "honesty" as a gendered concept). Smith is an American woman sentenced to life in prison for drowning her two children in 1995. Wuornos was an American woman sentenced to the death penalty for the murder of seven men between 1989 and 1990. She is frequently dubbed "the first female serial killer," because she was the first woman to be classified as such by the FBI. West is an English woman sentenced to life in prison in 1995 for her murder of ten people.

7 See Sarah VanHooser Suiter, *Magdalene House: A Place about Mercy* and http://www.npr.org/series/135746975/up-from-prostitution.

8 http://www.thistlefarms.org/index.php/about-magdalene.

9 http://www.thistlefarms.org/index.php/about-thistle-farms.

Appendix

1 Translation from Spanish to English is mine.

2 I purposefully leave all forms or the Spanish verb *recoger* untranslated here in order to demonstrate the multiple meanings of the word throughout the text. See the introduction for a longer explanation of this concept.

Works Cited

Acosta Africano, Cristóbal. *Tratado en loor de las mugeres y de la castidad, onestidad, constancia, silencio y justicia.* Venice: Presso Giacomo Cornetti, 1592.

Allen, John Jay. *The Reconstruction of a Spanish Golden-Age Playhouse.* Gainesville: U of Florida P, 1983.

Allen, John Jay, and José M. Ruana de la Haza. *Los teatros comerciales del siglo XVII y la escenificación de la comedia.* Madrid: Editorial Castalia, 1994.

Almeda, Elisabet. *Mujeres y castigo: Un enfoque socio-jurídico y de género.* Madrid: Editorial Dykinson, 2007.

– "Pasado y presente de las cárceles femeninas en España." *Sociológica* 6 (2005): 75–106.

Arenal, Electra, and Stacey Schlau. *Untold Sisters: Hispanic Nuns in Their Own Works.* Trans. Amanda Powell. Albuquerque: U of New Mexico P, 2009.

Armon, Shifra. *Picking Wedlock: Women and the Courtship Novel in Spain.* Oxford: Rowman & Littlefield, 2002.

Arrizabalaga, Jon, John Henderson, and Roger French. *The Great Pox: The French Disease in Renaissance Europe.* New Haven: Yale UP, 1997.

Astete, Gaspar de. *Tratado del govierno de la familia y estado de las viudas y doncellas.* Burgos: Compañía de Jesús, 1603.

Barahona, Renato. *Sex Crimes, Honour, and the Law in Early Modern Spain: Vizcaya, 1528–1735.* Toronto: U of Toronto P, 2003.

Barbeito Carneiro, María Isabel. *Cárceles y mujeres en el siglo XVII.* Madrid: Editorial Castalia, 1991.

– "Reliquias en textos y contextos femeninos." *Via spiritus* 8 (2001): 185–218.

Bass, Laura, and Amanda Wunder. "The Veiled Ladies of the Early Modern Spanish World: Seduction and Scandal in Seville, Madrid, and Lima." *Hispanic Review* 77.1 (winter 2009): 97–144.

Bayliss, Robert. "Feminism and María de Zayas's Exemplary Comedy, *La traición en la amistad.*" *Hispanic Review* 76.1 (winter 2008): 1–17.

Bilinkoff, Jodi. *Related Lives: Confessors and Their Female Penitents, 1450–1750.* Ithaca: Cornell UP, 2005.

Blue, William R. *Spanish Comedias and Historical Contexts in the 1620s.* University Park: Pennsylvania State UP, 1996.

Boyle, Margaret E. "Chronicling Women's Containment in Bartolomé Arzáns de Orsúa y Vela's *History of Potosí.*" *Studies in Eighteenth-Century Culture* 39 (2010): 279–96.

– "Inquisition and Epistolary Negotiation: Examining the Correspondence of Teresa de la Valle y la Cerda." *Letras Femeninas, Mujeres alborotadas: Early Modern and Colonial Women's Cultural Production: A Festschrift for Electa Arenal* 35.1 (2009): 293–309.

Breve Tratado de los Hospitales y Casas de Recogimiento, Agosto 1677. Biblioteca Nacional Madrid. Sig, 3/38623.

Brooks, Lynn. *The Dances of the Processions of Seville in Spain's Golden Age.* Kassel: Edition Reichenberger, 1988.

Brown, Jonathan, and J.H. Elliott. *A Palace for a King: The Buen Retiro and the Court of Philip IV.* New Haven: Yale UP, 1980.

Brownlee, Marina S. *The Cultural Labyrinth of Maria de Zayas.* Philadelphia: U of Pennsylvania P, 2000.

– "Permutations of the Narrator-Protagonist: The *Serrana* Episodes of the *Libro de buen amor* in Light of the Doña Endrina Sequence." *Romance Notes* 22.1 (1981): 98–101.

Butler, Judith. *Gender Trouble: Feminism and the Subversion of Identity.* New York: Routledge, 1990.

Caba, Maria Y. *Isabel La Católica en la producción teatral española del siglo XVII.* London: Tamesis, 2008.

Calderón de la Barca, Pedro. *La dama duende.* Madrid: Espasa-Calpe, 1973.

– *The Phantom Lady.* Ed. and trans. Donald Beecher and James Nelson Novoa. Ottawa: Dovehouse, 2002.

Campbell, Gwyn E. "(En)gendering Fenisa in Maria de Zayas's *La Traición en la amistad.*" *Romance Languages Annual* 10 (1999): 482–7.

Cañadas, Iván. *Public Theater in Golden Age Madrid and Tudor-Stuart London: Class, Gender and Festive Community.* Burlington, VT: Ashgate, 2005.

Capmany y Montopaulau, Antonio. *Orígen histórico y etimológico de las calles de Madrid.* Madrid: Imprenta de Manuel B. de Quirós, 1863.

Carmona García, Juan Ignacio. *Enfermedad y sociedad en los primeros tiempos modernos.* Seville: Universidad de Sevilla, 2005.

Carrión, Gabriela. *Staging Marriage in Early Modern Spain: Conjugal Doctrine in Lope, Cervantes, and Calderón.* Lewisburg, PA: Bucknell UP, 2011.

Carrión, María M. *Subject Stages: Marriage, Theatre and the Law in Early Modern Spain*. Toronto: U of Toronto P, 2010.

– "Here Comes the Real Bride: Anna de Austria and the Birth of Theatre in Early Modern Spain." *REH* 40 (2006): 113–44.

– "Portrait of a Lady: Marriage, Postponement, and Representation in Ana Caro's 'El Conde Partinuplés'." *MLN* 114.2 (1999): 241–68.

Cartagena Calderón, José Reinaldo. *Masculinidades en obras: El drama de la hombría en la España imperial*. Newark, DE: Juan de la Cuesta, 2008.

Carvajal y Mendoza, Luisa de. *This Tight Embrace*. Ed. and trans. Elizabeth Rhodes. Milwaukee, WI: Marquette UP, 2000.

Castro, Américo. *De la edad conflictiva: Crisis de la cultura española en el siglo XVII*. Madrid: Taurus, 1972.

Cerda, Juan de la. *Libro intitulado vida política de todos los estados de mugeres*. Alcalá de Henares: Casa de Juan Gracián, 1599.

Cháves, Cristóbal de. *Relación de la cárcel de Sevilla*. Madrid: Clásicos El Arbol, 1983.

Cohen, Gary B., and Franz A.J. Szabo. *Embodiments of Power: Building Baroque Cities in Europe*. New York: Berghahn Books, 2008.

Cohen, Sherrill. *The Evolution of Women's Asylums since 1500*. New York: Oxford UP, 1992.

Cotarelo y Mori, Emilio. "Actores famosos del siglo XVII: Sebastián de Prado y su mujer Bernarda Ramírez." *Boletín de la Real Academia Española* 2 (1915): 425–57.

– *Bibliografía de las controversias sobre la licitud del teatro en España*. Madrid: Est. de la "Rev. de archivos, bibliotecas y museos," 1904.

– *Luis Vélez de Guevara y sus obras dramáticas*, Alicante: Biblioteca Virtual Miguel de Cervantes, 2010. http://www.cervantesvirtual.com/FichaObra. html?Ref=37515.

Covarrubias Orozco, Sebastián de. *Tesoro de la lengua castellana o española*. Madrid: Editorial Castalia, 1994.

Crocetti, María Martino. "La dama duende: Spatial and Hymeneal Dialectics." Stoll and Smith 51–66.

Cruz, Anne J. *Discourses of Poverty: Social Reform and the Picaresque Novel in Early Modern Spain*. Toronto: U of Toronto P, 1999.

– "Willing Desire: Luisa de Carvajal y Mendoza and Female Subjectivity." *Power and Gender in Renaissance Spain*. Ed. Helen Nadar. Chicago: U of Illinois P, 2004. 177–94.

Cruz, Anne J., and Rosilie Hernández. *Women's Literacy in Early Modern Spain and the New World*. Burlington, VT: Ashgate UP, 2011.

Cruz, Anne J., and Mary Elizabeth Perry, eds. *Culture and Control in Counter Reformation Spain*. Minneapolis: U of Minnesota P, 1992.

Cruz, Anne J., and Mihoko Suzuki, eds. *The Rule of Women in Early Modern Europe*. Chicago: U of Illinois P, 2009.

Daniels, Mary Blythe. "Revisioning Gender on the Seventeenth-Century Spanish Stage: A Study of Actresses and Autoras." Dissertation, University of Kentucky, Lexington, 1998.

Dauge-Roth, Katherine L. "Textual Performance: Imprinting the Criminal Body." *Biblio: Intersections*. Ed. Faith E. Beasley and Kathleen Wine. Tübingen: Narr Francke Attempto, 2005. 125–43.

Davis, Natalie Z. *Fiction in the Archives: Pardon Tales and Their Tellers in Sixteenth-Century France*. Stanford: Stanford UP, 1987.

– *Trickster Travels: A Sixteenth-Century Muslim between Worlds*. London: Faber and Faber, 2008.

De Austria, Clara Isabel Eugenia. *Correspondencia de la Infanta Doña Clara Isabel Eugenia con el Duque de Lerma y otros personajes*. Madrid: Fortanet, 1906.

De Backer, Stephanie Fink. *Widowhood in Early Modern Spain: Protectors, Proprietors, and Patrons*. Leiden: Brill, 2010.

De Luján, Pedro. *Coloquios matrimoniales*. Madrid: Ediciones Atlas, 1943.

Domínguez Ortiz, Antonio. "La galera o cárcel de mujeres de Madrid a comienzos del siglo XVIII." *Anales del Instituto de Estudios Madrileños*. Madrid: Consejo Superior de Investigación, 1973. 277–85.

Donnell, Sidney. *Feminizing the Enemy: Imperial Spain, Transvestite Drama, and the Crisis of Masculinity*. Lewisburg, PA: Bucknell UP, 2003.

Dopico Black, Georgina. *Perfect Wives, Other Women: Adultery and Inquisition in Early Modern Spain*. Durham: Duke UP, 2001.

– "Public Bodies, Private Parts: The Virgins and Magdalens of Magdalena de San Gerónimo." *Journal of Spanish Cultural Studies* 2.1 (2001): 81–96.

Ehrenreich, Barbara. "Foreward: Feminism's Assumptions Upended." *One of the Guys: Women as Aggressors and Torturers*. Ed. Tara McKelvey. Emeryville, CA: Seal P, 2007. 1–7.

Elias, Norbert. *The Court Society*. Oxford: Basil Blackwell, 1983.

Elliott, J.H. "Power and Propaganda in the Spain of Philip IV." *Rites of Power: Symbolism, Ritual and Politics since the Middle Ages*. Ed. Sean Wilentz. Philadelphia: U of Pennsylvania P, 1999. 145–73.

Entrambasaguas, Joaquín de. *Estudios sobre Lope de Vega*. Madrid: Consejo Superior de Investigaciones Científicas, 1967.

Escritura de Cesión ortigada por la Madre San Jerónimo. Archivo Histórico Nacional Madrid. Sig. Clero, Secular-Regular Legajo, 17851. n.d.

Fernández Vargas, Valentina, and María Victoria López-Cordón Cortezo, "Mujer y régimen jurídico en el Antiguo Régimen: Una realidad disociada." *Ordenamiento jurídico y realidad social de las mujeres: Siglos XVI a XX*. Actas de las IV Jornadas de Investigación Interdisciplinaria. Seminario de Estudios de la Mujer. Universidad Autónoma de Madrid, 1986. 13–40.

Feros, Antonio. *Kingship and Favoritism in the Spain of Philip III, 1598–1621.* Cambridge: Cambridge UP, 2006.

Ferrer Valls, Teresa. *Diccionario biográfico de actores del teatro clásico español (DI-CAT).* Kassel: Edition Reichenberger, 2008.

– *Nobleza y espectáculo teatral, 1535–1622: Estudio y documentos.* Seville: Universidad de Sevilla, 1993.

Foucault, Michel. *Discipline and Punish: The Birth of the Prison.* Trans. Alan Sheridan. New York: Vintage Books, 1995.

Friedman, Ellen G. "El status jurídico de là mujer castellana durante el Antiguo Régimen." *Ordenamiento jurídico y realidad social de las mujeres: Siglos XVI a XX.* Ed. María Carmen García-Nieto. Madrid: Universidad Autónoma de Madrid, 1986. 41–53.

Frye, Susan, and Karen Robertson, eds. *Maids and Mistresses, Cousins and Queens: Women's Alliances in Early Modern England.* New York: Oxford UP, 1999.

Fundación y Patronato del Convento fundado por Madre San Jerónimo. Archivo Histórico Nacional Madrid. Sig. Clero Secular-Regular Legajo, 17295. n.d.

Galdiano y Croy, Leonardo. *Breve tratado de los hospitales y casas de recogimiento.* Madrid: La Imprenta Real, 1677.

Gamboa, Yolanda. "Architectural Cartography: Social and Gender Mapping in María de Zayas's Seventeenth-Century Spain." *Hispanic Review* 71.2 (spring 2003): 189–203.

– *Cartografía social en la narrativa de María de Zayas.* Madrid: Biblioteca Nueva, 2009.

Ganelin, Charles, and Howard Mancing. *The Golden Age Comedia: Text, Theory and Performance.* West Lafayette, IN: Purdue UP, 1994.

Gascón, Christopher D. *The Woman Saint in Spanish Golden Age Drama.* Lewisburg, PA: Bucknell UP, 2006.

Giles, Mary E. *Women in the Inquisition: Spain and the New World.* Baltimore: Johns Hopkins UP, 1998.

Goldberg, Jonathan. *Queering the Renaissance.* Durham: Duke UP, 1994.

Gorfkle, Laura. "Female Communities, Female Friendships and Social Control in María de Zayas's *La traición en la amistad*: A Historical Perspective." *Romance Languages Annual* 10 (1999): 615–20.

Gowing, Laura. *Common Bodies: Women, Touch and Power in Seventeenth-Century England.* New Haven: Yale UP, 2003.

– *Domestic Dangers: Women, Words, and Sex in Early Modern London.* New York: Oxford UP, 1996.

Gowing, Laura, Michael Hunter, and Miri Rubin, eds. *Love, Friendship and Faith in Europe, 1300–1800*. New York: Palgrave, 2005.

Grafton, Anthony. *What was History? The Art of History in Early Modern Europe*. Cambridge: Cambridge UP, 2007.

Greer, Margaret Rich. *María de Zayas Tells Baroque Tales of Love and the Cruelty of Men*. University Park: Pennsylvania State UP, 2000.

– "The (Self)-Representation of Control in *La dama duende*." *The Golden Age Comedia: Text, Theory, and Performance*. Ed. Charles Ganelin and Howard Mancing. West Lafayette, IN: Purdue UP, 1994. 87–106.

– "A Tale of Three Cities: The Place of Theatre in Early Modern Madrid, Paris and London." *Bulletin of Hispanic Studies* 77.1 (2000): 391–429.

Greer, Margaret Rich, Walter Mignolo, and Maureen Quilligan, eds. *Rereading the Black Legend: The Discourses of Religious and Racial Difference in the Renaissance Empires*. Chicago: U of Chicago P, 2007.

Halley, Janet. *Split Decisions: How and Why to Take a Break from Feminism*. Princeton: Princeton UP, 1998.

Hauer, Mary G. *Luis Vélez de Guevara: A Critical Bibliography*. Chapel Hill: U of North Carolina P, 1975.

Hesgtrom, Valerie. "The Fallacy of the False Dichotomy in María de Zayas's La traición en la amistad." Bulletin of the Comediantes 46.1 (1994): 59–70.

Herzog, Tamar. *Defining Nations: Immigrants and Citizens in Early Modern Spain and Spanish America*. New Haven: Yale UP, 2003.

Holmberg, Arthur. "Variaciones sobre el tema del honor en *La dama duende* de Calderón." *Calderón: Actas del Congreso internacional sobre Calderón y el teatro español del Siglo de Oro*. Ed. Luciano García Lorenzo. Madrid: Consejo Superior de Investigaciones Científicas, 1983. 913–23.

Joseph, Miranda. *Against the Romance of Community*. Minneapolis, MN: U of Minnesota P, 2002.

Kagan, Richard L. *Clio and the Crown: The Politics of History in Medieval and Early Modern Spain*. Baltimore: Johns Hopkins UP, 2009.

Kamen, Henry. *The Spanish Inquisition: A Historical Revision*. New Haven: Yale UP, 1998.

Kaminsky, Amy, ed. *Water Lilies: An Anthology of Spanish Women Writers from the Fifteenth through the Nineteenth Century*. Minneapolis: U of Minnesota P, 1996.

Kennedy, Ruth Lee. *Studies in Tirso*. Vol. 1, *The Dramatist and His Competitors (1620–26)*. Chapel Hill: U of North Carolina P, 1974.

Kuehn, Thomas. "Daughters, Mothers, Wives and Widows: Women as Legal Persons." *Time, Space, and Women's Lives in Early Modern Europe*. Ed. Anne Jacobson Schutte, Thomas Kuehn, and Silvana Seidel Menchi. Kirksville, MO: Truman State UP, 2001. 97–116.

Lacarra, María Eugenia. *El Poema de Mio Cid: Realidad histórica e ideología*. Madrid: J. Porrúa Turanzas, 1980.

Larson, Catherine. "*La dama duende* and the Shifting Characterization of Calderón's Diabolical Angel." Stoll and Smith 33–51.

– *Language and the Comedia: Theory and Practice*. Lewisburg, PA: Bucknell UP, 1991.

Laskier Martín, Adrienne. *An Erotic Philology of Golden Age Spain*. Nashville, TN: Vanderbilt UP, 2008.

Lazar, Gabriel Lance. *Working in the Vineyard of the Lord: Jesuit Confraternities in Early Modern Italy*. Toronto: U of Toronto P, 2005.

Lehfeldt, Elizabeth. *Religious Women in Golden Age Spain: The Permeable Cloister*. Burlington: Ashgate, 2005.

León, Fray Luis de. *La perfecta casada*. Ed. and trans. John A. Jones and Javier San José Lera. Lewiston, NY: Edwin Mellen P, 1999.

Lerner, Gerda. *The Creation of Patriarchy*. New York: Oxford UP, 1986.

Levy, Allison M. *Widowhood and Visual Culture in Early Modern Europe*. Burlington, VT: Ashgate, 2003.

Lope de Vega, Félix. *El castigo sin venganza*. Ed. Antonio Carreño. Madrid: Cátedra, 2006.

López Martínez, Celestino. *Teatros y comediantes sevillanos del siglo XVI*. Seville: Imprenta Provincial, 1940.

Lundelius, Ruth. "Paradox and Role Reversal in *La serrana de la Vera*." Stoll and Smith 220–44.

Malón de Chaide, Pedro. *La conversión de la Magdalena*. Ed. P. Félix García. Madrid: Espasa-Calpe, 1957.

Maravall, José Antonio. *Teatro y literatura en la sociedad barroca*. Madrid: Editorial Critica, 1990.

Mariscal, George. *Contradictory Subjects: Quevedo, Cervantes, and Seventeenth-Century Spanish Culture*. Ithaca: Cornell UP, 1998.

Maroto Camino, Mercedes. "Maria de Zayas and Ana Caro: The Space of Woman's Solidarity in the Spanish Golden Age." *Hispanic Review* 67.1 (1999): 1–16.

Martínez Galindo, Gema. *Galerianas, corrigendas y presas: Nacimiento y consolidación de las cárceles de mujeres en España (1608–1913)*. Madrid: Edisofer, 2002.

McGinley, Ann C. "Hillary Clinton, Sarah Palin, and Michelle Obama: Performing Gender, Race, and Class on the Campaign Trail." *Denver University Law Review* 86 (2009): 709–25.

McKendrick, Melveena. *Identities in Crisis: Essays on Honour, Gender and Women in the Comedia*. Kassel, Germany: Edition Reichberger, 2002.

– "Representing Their Sex: Actresses in Seventeenth-Century Spain." *Rhetoric and Reality in Early Modern Spain*. Ed. Richard J. Pym. London: Tamesis, 2006. 72–92.

– *Theatre in Spain, 1490–1700*. Cambridge: Cambridge UP, 1989.

– *Woman and Society in the Spanish Drama of the Golden Age: A Study of the Mujer Varonil*. London: Cambridge UP, 1974.

– "Women against Wedlock: The Reluctant Brides of Spain's Golden Age." *Women in Hispanic Literature: Icons and Fallen Idols*. Ed. Beth Miller. Berkeley: U of California P, 1983. 115–46.

Meijide Pardo, María Luisa. *La mujer de la orilla: Visión histórica de la mendiga y prostituta en las cárceles galeras de hace dos siglos*. Sada: Edicios de Castro, 1996.

Mérimée, Henri. *Spectacles et comediens á Valencia (1580–1630)*. Toulouse and Paris: Edouard Privat-Auguste Picard, 1913.

Merrim, Stephanie. *Early Modern Women's Writing and Sor Juana Inés de la Cruz*. Nashville, TN: Vanderbilt UP, 1999.

Mirrer, Louise, ed. *Upon My Husband's Death: Widows in the Literature and Histories of Medieval Europe*. Ann Arbor: U of Michigan P, 1992.

Molina, Tirso de. *El burlador de Sevilla*. Ed. Alfredo Rodríguez López-Vázquez. Madrid: Cátedra, 1990.

Moreiras, Alberto. "Spanish Nation Formation: An Introduction." *Journal of Spanish Cultural Studies* 2.1 (2001): 5–11.

Moreno Sardà, Amparo. *La otra política de Aristóteles: Cultura de masas y divulgación del arquetipo viril*. Barcelona: Editorial Icaria, 1988.

Mujica, Bárbara, *Calderón's Characters: An Existential Point of View*. Barcelona: Puvill-Editor, 1980.

– "Tragic Elements in Calderón's *La dama duende*." *Kentucky Romance Quarterly* 16 (1969): 303–28.

– ed. *Women Writers of Early Modern Spain: Sophia's Daughters*. New Haven: Yale UP, 2004.

Muñoz Fernández, Ángela. *Acciones e intenciones de mujeres: Vida religiosa de las madrileñas*. Madrid: Horas y Horas, 1995.

Muriel, Josefina. *Los recogimientos de mujeres: Respuesta a una problemática social novohispana*. Mexico: Universidad Nacional Autónoma de México, 1974.

Nauert, Charles Garfield. *Humanism and the Culture of Renaissance Europe*. Cambridge: Cambridge UP, 2006.

O'Connor, Thomas Austin. *Love in the "Corral": Conjugal Spirituality and Antitheatrical Polemic in Early Modern Spain*. New York: Peter Lang, 2001.

Oehrlein, Joseph. *El actor en el teatro español del Siglo de Oro*. Madrid: Editorial Castalia, 1993.

Olivares, Julián, and Elizabeth S. Boyce, eds. *Tras el espejo la musa escribe: Lírica femenina de los Siglos de Oro*. Madrid: Siglo Veintiuno, 1993.

Ordóñez, Pedro José. *Monvmento trivnfal de la piedad catolica: Ó sea, Del recogimiento de los Mendigos y expulsion de los vagamundos, 1673*. Biblioteca Nacional Madrid. Sig. 3/4616. n.d.

Parker, Alexander A. *La filosofía del amor en la literatura española: 1480–1680*. Madrid: Cátedra, 1986.

Parr, James A. "Some Remarks on Tragedy and on Vélez as a Tragedian: A Response to Professor Whitby." *Antigüedad y actualidad de Luis Vélez de Guevara*. Ed. C. George Peale. Philadelphia: John Benjamins, 1983. 137–43.

Paun de García, Susan. "Zayas as Writer: Hell Hath No Fury." *María de Zayas: The Dynamics of Discourse*. Ed. Amy R. Williamsen and Judith A. Whitenack. Cranbury, NJ: Associated UP, 1995. 40–51.

Pellicer, Casiano. *Tratado histórico sobre el origen y progreso de la comedia y del histrionismo en España*. 2 vols. Madrid: Imprenta de la Administración del Real Arbitrio de Beneficencia, 1804.

Peña, Mercedes de los Reyes. "En torno a la actriz Jusepa Vaca." *Las mujeres en la sociedad Española del Siglo de Oro: Ficción teatral y realidad histórica*. Ed. Pilar Ballarín Domingo. Granada: Aula Biblioteca, 1997; Granada: U de Granada P, 1998. 81–114.

Pérez Baltasar, María Dolores. "El castigo del delito: Galeras y recogimientos para la mujer pública en el Madrid de los siglos XVII y XVIII." *Espacios y mujeres*. Málaga: Universidad de Málaga, 2006.

– *Mujeres marginadas: Las casas de recogidas en Madrid*. Madrid: Gráficas Lormo, 1984.

Pérez de Colosía Rodríguez, María Isabel. "Mujeres procesadas por el tribunal del santo oficio de Granada." *Baetica* 27 (2005): 423–36.

– "La mujer y el Santo Oficio de Granada durante la segunda mitad del siglo XVI." *Ordenamiento jurídico y realidad social de las mujeres: Siglos XVI a XX*. Ed. María Carmen García-Nieto. Madrid: Universidad Autónoma de Madrid, 1986. 55–70.

Pérez de Herrera, Cristóbal. *Del amparo y reformacion de los fingidos vagabundos*. Madrid: Espasa-Calpe, 1975.

Pérez de Valdivia, Diego. *Aviso de gente recogida*. Salamanca: Universidad Pontificia de Salamanca, 1977.

Perry, Mary Elizabeth. *Crime and Society in Early Modern Seville*. Hanover, NH: UP of New England, 1980.

– "Deviant Insiders: Legalized Prostitutes and a Consciousness of Women in Early Modern Seville." *Comparative Studies in Society and History* 27.1 (January 1985): 138–58.

- *Gender and Disorder in Early Modern Seville*. Princeton: Princeton UP, 1990.
- "With Brave Vigilance and a Hundred Eyes: The Making of Women's Prisons in Counter-Reformation Spain." *Women & Criminal Justice* 2.1 (1991): 3–17.

Pike, Ruth. *Penal Servitude in Early Modern Spain*. Madison: U of Wisconsin P, 1983.

Poska, Allyson M. *Women and Authority in Early Modern Spain: The Peasants of Galicia*. Oxford: Oxford UP, 2005.

Postigo Castellanos, Elena. *Honor y privilegio en la Corona de Castilla: El Consejo de las Órdenes y los Caballeros de hábito en el siglo XVII*. Valladolid: Junta de Castilla y León, 1988.

Pym, Richard J. *Rhetoric and Reality in Early Modern Spain*. London: Tamesis, 2006.

Rambuss, Richard. *Closet Devotions*. Durham: Duke UP, 1998.

Ramón Laca, Julio de. *Las viejas cárceles madrileñas: Siglos XV y XIX*. Madrid: Delegación de Educación, Instituto de Estudios Madrileños, 1973.

Recio, Manuel. *Compendio histórico, y manifiesto instructivo del origen, y fundación de la Real Casa de Santa Maria Magdalena de la Penitencia, vulgo las Recogidas de Madrid, declarándose también sus rentas, y efectos, los patronatos, y memorias fundadas en su Iglesia, los Señores Protectores*. Biblioteca Nacional Madrid. Sig. R/39310 fols. 196. n.d.

Rennert, Hugo. *The Life of Lope de Vega, 1562–1635*. New York: Arno Press, 1968.

- *The Spanish Stage in the Time of Lope de Vega*. New York: The Hispanic Society of America, 1909.

Ringrose, David. "Madrid: Capital Imperial (1561–1833)." *Madrid: Historia de una capital*. Ed. Santos Juliá, David Ringrose, and Cristina Segura. Madrid: Alianza, 1994. 123–251.

Romero-Díaz, Nieves. *Nueva nobleza, nueva novela: reescribiendo la cultura urbana del barroco*. Madrid: Juan de la Cuesta, 2002.

Ruano de la Haza, J.M. "The Staging of Calderón's *La vida es sueño* and *La dama duende*." *Bulletin of Hispanic Studies* 64 (1987): 51–63.

Ruiz, Teófilio F. *A King Travels: Festive Traditions in Late Medieval and Early Modern Spain*. Princeton: Princeton UP, 2012.

Sánchez, Magdalena S. *The Empress, the Queen, and the Nun: Women and Power in the Court of Philip III of Spain*. Baltimore: Johns Hopkins UP, 1998.

- "Sword and Wimple: Isabel Clara Eugenia and Power." Cruz and Suzuki 64–79.

Sánchez, Magdalena S., and Alain Saint-Saëns. *Spanish Women in the Golden Age: Images and Realities*. Westport, CT: Greenwood P, 1996.

Sánchez Arjona, José. *Noticias referentes a los anales del teatro en Sevilla desde Lope de Rueda hasta fines del siglo XVII*. Seville: E. Rasco, 1898.

Sánchez Ortega, María Helena. *Pecadoras en verano, arrepentidas en invierno: El camino de la conversión femenina*. Madrid: Alianza, 2005.

– "Woman as Source of 'Evil' in Counter-Reformation Spain." Trans. Susan Isabel Stein. *Culture and Control in Counter-Reformation Spain*. Ed. Anne J. Cruz and Mary Elizabeth Perry. Minneapolis: U of Minnesota P, 1992. 196–215.

San Jerónimo, Magdalena de. "Razón y forma de la galera y casa real." *Cárceles y mujeres en el siglo XVII*. Ed. Barbeito Carniero 61–95.

Santo-Tomás, Enrique García. *El teatro del Siglo de Oro ante los espacios de la crítica: Encuentros y revisions*. Madrid: Iberoamericana, 2002.

Schlau, Stacey. *Gendered Crime and Punishment: Women and/in the Hispanic Inquisitions*. Leiden: Brill, 2012.

Scott, Joan Wallach. *Gender and the Politics of History*. New York: Columbia UP, 1988.

– "Gender: A Useful Category of Historical Analysis." *The American Historical Review* 91.5 (December 1986): 1053–75.

Sellers, Alicia Álvarez. *Del texto a la iconografía: Aproximación al document teatral del siglo XVII*. Valencia: Publicacions de la Universitat de Valéncia, 2007.

Shergold, N.D. *A History of the Spanish Stage: From Medieval Times until the End of the Seventeenth Century*. Oxford: Clarendon P, 1967.

Shergold, N.D., and J.E. Varey. *Fuentes para la historia del teatro en España*. 2 vols. London: Tamesis, 1985.

Siena, Kevin P. *Venereal Disease, Hospitals and the Urban Poor: London's "Foul Wards" (1600–1800)*. Rochester, NY: U of Rochester P, 2004.

Sjoberg, Laura, and Caron E. Gentry. *Mothers, Monsters, Whores: Women's Violence in Global Politics*. London: Zed Books, 2007.

Socolow, Susan. *The Women of Colonial Latin America*. New York: Cambridge UP, 2000.

Soufas, Teresa Scott, ed. *Women's Acts: Plays by Women Dramatists of Spain's Golden Age*. Lexington: UP of Kentucky, 1997.

Stoll, Anita K., and Dawn L. Smith, eds. *Gender, Identity and Representation in Spain's Golden Age*. Cranbury, NJ: Associated UP, 2000.

– eds. *The Perception of Women in Spanish Theater of the Golden Age*. Cranbury, NJ: Associated UP, 1991.

Stradling, R.A. *Philip IV and the Government of Spain, 1621–1665*. Cambridge: Cambridge UP, 2002.

Strocchia, Sharon T. "Taken into Custody: Girls and Convent Guardianship in Renaissance Florence." *Renaissance Studies* 17.2 (2003): 177–200.

Strother, Darci L. "Constructing a Goddess: Gila's Role in Vélez de Guevara's *La serrana de la Vera*." *A Star-crossed Golden Age: Myth and the Spanish*

Comedia. Ed. Frederick A. De Armas. Lewisburg, PA: Bucknell UP, 1998. 162–76.

Stroud, Matthew D. "Homo/Hetero/Social/Sexual: Gila in Vélez's 'La serrana de la Vera.'" *Golden Age Studies in Memory of Daniel L. Heiple*. Ed. Julián Olivares. Special issue of *Calíope* 6.1–2 (2000): 53–69.

– "Love, Friendship, and Deceit in *La traición en la amistad* by María de Zayas." *Neophilologus* 69 (1985): 539–47.

– *Plot Twists and Critical Turns: Queer Approaches to Early Modern Spanish Theater*. Lewisburg, PA: Bucknell UP, 2007.

Suárez de Figueroa, Cristóbal. *Plaza universal de todas ciencias y artes*. Madrid: Luis Sánchez, 1615.

Terpstra, Nicolas. *Abandoned Children of the Italian Renaissance: Orphan Care in Florence and Bologna*. Baltimore: Johns Hopkins UP, 2005.

– "Mothers, Sisters and Daughters: Girls and Conservatory Guardianship in Late Renaissance Florence." *Renaissance Studies* 17.2 (2003): 201–29.

Thacker, Jonathan. *Role-Play and the World as Stage in the Comedia*. Liverpool: Liverpool UP, 2002.

Tikoff, Valentina K. "Gender and Juvenile Charity, Tradition and Reform: Assistance for Young People in Eighteenth-Century Seville." *Eighteenth Century Studies* 41.3 (2008): 307–35.

Tómas y Valiente, Francisco, ed. *Sexo barroco y otras transgresiones premodernas*. Madrid: Alianza, 2007.

Tormo, Elías. *En las Descalzas Reales, estudios históricos, iconográficos y artísticos*. Madrid: Blass y Cia, 1927.

Tsuchiya, Akiko. *Marginal Subjects: Gender and Deviance in Fin-de-siécle Spain*. Toronto: U of Toronto P, 2011.

Tuana, Nancy. *The Less Noble Sex: Scientific, Religious and Philosophical Conceptions of Woman's Nature*. Indianapolis: Indiana UP, 1993.

Van Deusen, Nancy E. *Between the Sacred and the Worldly: The Institutional and Cultural Practice of Recogimiento in Colonial Lima*. Stanford: Stanford UP, 2001.

VanHooser Suiter, Sarah. *Magdalene House: A Place about Mercy*. Nashville, TN: Vanderbilt UP, 2012.

Varey, J.E., and Charles J. Davis. *Los arriendos de los corrales de comedias de Madrid: 1587–1719: Estudio y documentos: Fuentes para la historia del teatro en España*. London: Tamesis, 1987.

– *Los corrales de comedias y los hospitales de Madrid: 1547–1615: Estudio y documentos: Fuentes para la historia del teatro en España*. London: Tamesis, 1997.

– *Los corrales de comedias y los hospitales de Madrid: 1615–1849: Estudio y documentos: Fuentes para la historia del teatro en España*. London: Tamesis, 1997.

Varey, J.E., Charles J. Davis, and Luciano García Lorenzo. *Teatros y vida teatral en el Siglo de Oro a través de las fuentes documentales*. London: Tamesis, 1991.

Varey, J.E., Charles J. Davis, and Margaret Rich Greer. *El teatro palaciego en Madrid, 1586–1707: Estudio y document: Fuentes para la historia del teatro en España*. Madrid: Tamesis, 1997.

Vázquez González, María Dolores. *Las cárceles de Madrid en el siglo XVII*. Madrid: Universidad Complutense de Madrid, 1992.

Velasco, Sherry. *Lesbians in Early Modern Spain*. Nashville, TN: Vanderbilt UP, 2011.

– *Male Delivery: Reproduction, Effeminacy, and Pregnant Men in Early Modern Spain*. Nashville, TN: Vanderbilt UP, 2006.

– *"Marimachos, hombrunas, barbudas:* The Masculine Woman in Cervantes." *Cervantes: Bulletin of the Cervantes Society of America* 20.1 (2000): 69–78.

Vélez de Guevara, Luis. *La serrana de la Vera*. Ed. William R. Mason and C. George Peale. Newark: Juan de la Cuesta, 2002.

– *La serrana de la Vera*. Ed. Enrique Rodríguez Cepeda. Madrid: Cátedra, 1982.

Villalba Pérez, Enrique. *La administración de la justicia penal en Castilla y en la Corte a comienzos del Siglo XVII*. Madrid: Actas, 1993.

– *Mujeres y orden social en Madrid: Delincuencia femenina en el cambio de coyuntura finisecular (1580–1630)*. Madrid: Editorial de la Universidad Complutense de Madrid, 1993.

Villamediana, Juan de Tassis y Peralta. *Obras*. Ed. Juan Manuel Rozas. Madrid: Claásicos Castalia, 1969.

Vives, Juan Luis. *De institutione feminae christianae*. Ed and trans. Charles Fantazzi. Chicago: U of Chicago P, 2000.

Vollendorf, Lisa. "Desire Unbound: Women's Theater of Spain's Golden Age." *Women in the Discourse of Early Modern Spain*. Ed. Joan F. Cammarata. Gainesville: U of Florida P, 2003. 272–93.

– *The Lives of Women: A New History of Inquisitional Spain*. Nashville, TN: Vanderbilt UP, 2005.

– *Reclaiming the Body: María de Zayas' Early Modern Feminism*. Chapel Hill: U of North Carolina P, 2001.

– "The Value of Female Friendship in Seventeenth-Century Spain." *Texas Studies in Literature and Language* 47.4 (2000): 425–45.

Weissberger, Barbara F. *Isabel Rules: Constructing Queenship, Wielding Power*. Minneapolis: U of Minnesota P, 2004.

– *"Tanto monta*: The Catholic Monarchs' Nuptial Fiction and the Power of Isabel I of Castile." Cruz and Suzuki 43–64.

Whitby, William M. "Some Thoughts on Vélez as a Tragedian." *Antigüedad y actualidad de Luis Vélez de Guevara*. Ed. C. George Peale. Philadelphia: Johns Benjamins, 1983. 127–37.

Wiesner-Hanks, Merry E. *Women and Gender in Early Modern Europe*. Cambridge: Cambridge UP, 2008.

Wilkins, Constance. "Subversion through Comedy? Two Plays by Sor Juana Inés de la Cruz and María de Zayas." Stoll and Smith 107–20.

Williamsen, Amy, and Judith A. Whitenack. *María de Zayas and the Dynamics of Discourse*. London: Associated UP, 1995.

Yagüe Olmos, Concepción. *Madres en prisión: Historia de las cárceles de mujeres a través de su vertiente maternal*. Granada: Editorial Comares, 2007.

Ynduráin, Domingo. *Humanismo y renacimiento en España*. Madrid: Cátedra, 1994.

Zayas, María de. "La traición en la amistad." *Women's Acts: Plays by Women Dramatists of Spain's Golden Age*. Ed. Teresa Scott Soufas. Lexington: UP of Kentucky, 1997: 277–326.

– *La traición en la amistad*. Ed. Valerie Hegstrom. Trans. Catherine Larson. Cranbury, NJ: Associated UP, 1999.

Index

Acevedo, Fernando de (archbishop), 119

actresses: biographies of, 128n14; and celebrity gossip, 102; and class, 9–10; and greed, 10, 129n20; and income, 9, 129n19; and legal permission to act, 8, 53; and prostitutes, 11; and *La serrana de la Vera*, 78–9; and sexuality, 82; and sin, 5; societal roles of, 53; and sumptuary laws, 9–10; and widows, 49, 53; and women's communities, 66. *See also names of specific actresses*; performers

adultery, 47, 131n8, 139n12

agency: and La dama duende, 53–9; and gender, 87; and modern criminals, 103, 143n5; and *La serrana de la Vera*, 87

Agreda, María de Jesús, 134n24

Agueda, María, 10

Alegoría de la Vanidad, 11, 129nn22, 23

Alemán, Mateo, 138n1

Almeda, Elisabet, 4–5, 30

Del amparo y reformacion de los fingidos vagabundos (Pérez de Herrara), 132–3n16

Ana de Jesús, 30

Andía (marquis), 122

Andres de los Elgueros, 39–40

Anzaldúa, Gloría, 140n14

Arias, Gabriel, 121

Arrizabalaga, Jon, 132n14

Arthur (king), 84

Astete, Gaspar de, 5, 50

auto de fe, 6–7, 20–1, 89, 94, 128n11, 130n1

Auto de fe en la Plaza Mayor de Madrid (Rizzi), 130

Azevedo, Angela de, 137–8n1

Baltasar Carlos (prince), 135n1

Baltasara de los Reyes, Francisca, 10, 11, 100, 129n24

Barahona, Renato, 142n12

Barasa, María de, 137–8n1

Barbeito Carniero, María, 30, 133–4n21

Bass, Laura, 50

Bayliss, Robert, 138–9n6

beaterios, 22

Beecher, Donald, 135n1

betrayal: and *La dama duende*, 137n12; and *La serrana de la Vera*, 77, 80–1,

88–92, 142nn11, 12; and *La traición en la amistad*, 62, 66–7, 73

blindness, 66–7

Boleyn, Anne (character), 78

branding, 36–7, 135n30

Brooks, Lynn, 53, 132n10

Brownlee, Marina S., 137–8n1

Butler, Judith, 101

Caba, María Y., 141n9

Calderón, María Inés ("La Calderona"), 10–11, 129n23

Calderón de la Barca, Pedro: career of, 135nn1, 2; and *La cisma de Inglaterra*, 78; and *La hija del aire*, 78; and *El medico de su honra*, 78; and wife-murder plays, 78. See also *dama duende, La* (Calderón)

Campbell, Gwyn E., 63, 64

Cañadas, Iván, 142n11

Cano, Alonso, 121

Capmany y Montopaulau, Antonio, 27

Carmona García, Juan Ignacio, 132n14

Caro Mallén de Soto, Ana, 77–8, 137–8n1

Carreño de Miranda, Juan, 40, 121

Carvajal y Mendoza, Luisa de, 30, 31, 133–4n21, 134nn23, 24

casa de recogidas. See Magdalen houses

Casa de Santa María Magdalena de la Penitencia, La: and education, 26; and exemplarity, 19–20; and funding, 28; and *la galera*, 130n26; and marriage, 26–7; and Mary Magdalene, 39–40; and performance, 19–21, 28–9; and prostitutes, 25; and Recio's

manual, 25–9, 133n17, 134n25; and *recogimiento*, 21, 26–9, 40, 98–9; and rehabilitation, 19–21; and religious life, 26–7, 133n18; and same-sex relations, 133n19; site of, 27–8. *See also* Magdalen houses

Casa Pía de Arrepentidas de Santa Magdalena, 30

Cascales, Francisco de, 80

Castellar (marchioness), 65–6

celebrities, 102–3

Celestina, La (Fernando de Rojas), 62

Centurion, Octavio, 119

Cepeda, Enrique Rodríguez, 141n3

Cervantes, Miguel de, 137–8n1

Chaves, Cristóbal de, 133n19

children, 22, 111, 132n10

class: and actresses, 9–10, 82; and *La serrana de la Vera*, 84–7, 91, 142n11

clothing: and *auto de fe*, 128n11, 130n1; and betrayal, 137n12; and La Casa de Santa María Magdalena de la Penitencia, 28–9; and cross-dressing, 3; and *La dama duende*, 50, 56, 58, 137n12; and *la galera*, 35; and income, 9, 129n19; and masculine disguise, 77–8; and *La serrana de la Vera*, 87; and sumptuary laws, 9–10; and widows, 56

Coello, Antonio, 11

Cohen, Gary B., 132n13

comedia: about, 5–8; *comedia de enredo* (comedy of errors) 74, 80; and female playwrights, 62–3, 137–8n1; and Queen Isabel as character, 141n9; and rehabilitation, 7, 13–16, 41–2, 53, 93–4, 98–9, 101; and social norms, 46–7, 60–1, 75, 77, 80, 97–8; and staging of femicide, 78; and tricksters, 45. *See also* theatre

Compendio histórico ... (Recio), 25–9, 133n17, 134n25

confession, 29, 39–40, 57, 89, 93. *See also* conversion

Confradía de la Vera-Cruz, La, 27

containment: and betrayal, 68; and *La dama duende*, 46, 47, 49–55, 57–8, 60, 97; forms of, 67; and *la galera*, 36, 67; and Magdalena de Guzmán, 65–6; and Magdalen houses, 67; and marriage, 52; and punishment, 65–6, 67; and *La serrana de la Vera*, 84, 87; and *La traición en la amistad*, 76, 97. See also *recogimiento*

Contresras, Antonio de, 120

Contresras, Francisco de, 28, 120

conversion: and imagery, 40–1; and performance, 20, 100; and rehabilitation, 10–11; and *La serrana de la Vera*, 93–4; and sexuality, 29. *See also* confession

Coronel, Agustin, 3

Coronel, Barbara, 3–4

Coronel, Maria, 3

Cotarelo y Mori, Emilio, 8–9, 78, 128n8, 129n16, 140n1

courtesans. *See* prostitutes

courtly love, 140–1n2

Covarrubias Orozco, Sebastián de, 21, 36–7, 66–7, 71

Crocetti, María Martino, 136n10

cross-dressing, 3, 77–8

Cruz, Anne J., 20, 23, 24, 134n24

Cuevas, Eugenio de las, 129n22

Cueva y Silva, Leonor de la, 137–8n1

custodial institutions: and children, 111; and criminals, 132–3n16;

defined, 127n2; and education, 6, 26, 128n10; functions of, 5–6, 22; and funding, 5, 27, 28, 33, 99, 135n28; goals of, 4, 6; and performance, 15, 98; and prostitutes, 24; and punishment, 6; and the Recogidas of Madrid, 119–22; and *recogimiento*, 22; and rehabilitation, 4; and theatre, 4–6, 11, 99; types of, 4, 99–100; and unruly women, 98; and workhouses, 33, 135n28. *See also* Magdalen houses

dama duende, La (Calderón): and agency, 53–9; and clothing, 50, 56, 58, 137n12; and containment, 46, 47, 49–55, 57–8, 60, 97; and economic problems, 47–8, 60, 136n4; first performance of, 135n1; and frivolity, 57; and the glass cabinet, 52–3, 136n10; and marriage, 46, 52, 59–61, 97; and performance, 55–7, 137n11; popularity of, 135n2; and rehabilitation, 13, 45, 48, 53, 58–61, 97; and sexuality, 53, 55–6, 57–8; and social norms, 97; and theatre, 13, 46, 50–6, 60–1; themes of, 46–7; and unruly women, 13, 58–61; and widow, 13; and women's communities, 53–7. *See also* Calderón de la Barca, Pedro; widows

dama duende, La (Calderón) (by character): Ángela, 13, 45–61, 97, 136nn3, 9, 137nn11, 12; Beatriz, 55–7, 136n9; Cosme, 49–50, 55, 60, 137n11; Isabel, 48–9, 53–4; Luis, 53, 55, 57, 59, 60, 136n9; Manuel, 13, 49, 51, 53–6, 59, 136n9, 137n11; Rodrigo, 136n9

Daniels, Mary Blythe, 9, 11, 66, 129n19

Dauge-Roth, Katherine L., 37, 135n30

Davis, Charles J., 28

Davis, Natalie Z., 99

de Austria, Juan José, 129n22

De Backer, Stephanie Fink, 46, 48, 136n6

Delicado, 62

Desengaños amorosos (Zayas), 137–8n1, 138nn4, 5, 8

deviant women. *See* unruly women

Diaz, Tomas, 3

disease. *See* human health

Dopico Black, Georgina, 5, 30, 129n18

economic issues: about the crisis, 23, 132n11, 136n4; and *La dama duende*, 47–8, 60; and employment, 110; and false beggars, 34, 110–11, 135n29; and moral issues, 40–1; and poverty, 5, 22, 89, 131n7; and widows, 47; and women, 22, 131n6

education: and La Casa de Santa María Magdalena de la Penitencia, 26; and custodial institutions, 6, 128n10; and marriage, 86–7; and orphaned girls, 111; and theatre, 8; and women, 6. *See also* exemplarity

Ehrenreich, Barbara, 103

Elgueros, Andres de los, 121

Entrambasaguas, Joaquín de, 129n20

Escudo, Teresa, 10

esturpo. *See* violence

ethnic minorities: and disease, 132n14; and immigration, 23; and

moral behaviour, 5; and sexuality, 99–100

exemplarity: and La Casa de Santa María Magdalena de la Penitencia, 19–20; and custodial institutions, 98; and *la galera*, 38; and good women, 34; and Jusepa Vaca, 95; and Magdalen houses, 20; and modern celebrities, 102; and performance, 21; and punishment, 38, 67; and *recogimiento*, 21–2; and *La serrana de la Vera*, 14, 80–1, 84, 87–8, 93–5, 97; and theatre, 8, 20; and *La traición en la amistad*, 63, 97; and unruly women, 98; and women, 12, 34, 35. *See also* education; performance

false beggars, 34, 110–11, 135n29

Felipe II (king), 23, 30, 132n12

Felipe III (king), 23, 30, 32, 132–3n16, 133–4n21

Felipe IV (king), 12, 23, 120, 135n1

female deviance. *See* unruly women

Fernando (king), 141–2n10; as character, 14, 86, 89–90, 92, 94

festivals, 19–20, 81

Fomperosa y Quintana, Pedro, 8–9

Foucault, Michel, 6, 7, 25

French, Roger, 132n14

Galdiano y Croy, Leonardo, 33

galera, la: administration of, 33; and branding, 36; and La Casa de Santa María Magdalena de la Penitencia, 130n26; and clothing, 35; and containment, 36, 67; creation of, 30–1, 33–4, 134nn22, 25, 134–5n26; and criminal sentences, 33, 135n27; and daily routine, 38; and exemplarity, 38; and funding, 33, 135n28; goals of, 38–9; need for, 25, 32–3, 107–12, 132–3n16; and performance, 36–8; physical complex of, 35–6; and prostitutes, 34–5, 109–10; and punishment, 12–13, 30, 37–8, 39, 107, 109; and *recogimiento*, 98–9; and rehabilitation, 30–1, 33, 34, 38–9; and word "*galera*," 37; and workhouses, 33, 135n28. *See also* penitentiaries

Gamboa, Yolanda, 137–8n1

Gascón, Christopher D., 142n14

gender: and female politicians, 102; and gendered spaces, 52–3, 136n10; and gender relations, 39; and masculine disguise, 77–8; and masculine roles, 96; and the masculine woman, 3, 81–5, 91, 140–1n2; and moral behaviour, 4–5; and punishment, 30–2, 37; and rehabilitation, 40; and sentences, 135n27; and *La serrana de la Vera*, 87; and sexuality, 63; and social norms, 97; and *La traición en la amistad*, 138–9n6; and violence, 90, 92, 143n6. *See also* women

Gentry, Caron E., 104

Góngora, Luis de, 141n3

Gonzalez, Josef, 120

Gorfkle, Laura, 63, 65

Gowing, Laura, 51, 64

Grandezas de Madrid (Quintana), 133n18

Greco, Dominico, 121

greed, 10, 129n20

Greer, Margaret Rich, 41, 47, 136n4

Guevara, María de, 134n24

Guzmán, Feliciana Enríquez de, 137–8n1

Guzmán, Magdalena de, 65–6

Halley, Janet, 75

Hegstrom, Valerie, 63

Henderson, John, 132n14

Henry VIII (king) (character), 78

Heredia, María de, 128n14

Hernández, Isabel, 10

Herzog, Tamar, 100

Holmberg, Arthur, 46

hooks, bell, 140n14

hospitals: and La Confradía de la Vera-Cruz, 27; functions of, 131n4; and the Hospital de Peregrinos, 27; and *recogimiento*, 22

human health: and ethnic minorities, 132n14; and moral behaviour, 128n9; and prostitutes, 110; and punishment, 6

Ibañez de la Riva Herrera, Antonio (archbishop), 122

iconography: and Mary Magdalene, 11, 40; and piercing arrows, 94, 142n15; and theatre, 129n23

income, 5, 9–10, 99, 110, 129n20

Inquisition: and *auto de fe*, 6–7, 20–1, 128n11, 130n1; and moral behaviour, 22; and performance, 3, 41

Isabel (queen), 30, 141n9, 141–2n10; as character in *La serrana de la Vera*, 14, 85–6, 88, 90, 92. *See also* royal women

Isabel Clara Eugenia de Austria (infanta), 30, 31
isolation. *See* containment

Jacinta, Mariana, 53
Jalon, Francisco, 3
Joseph, Miranda, 75–6, 140n14

Kagan, Richard L., 134n25
Kamen, Henry, 7, 20–1
Kuehn, Thomas, 48

Larson, Catherine, 46–7, 63, 139n11
Laskier Martín, Adrienne, 140–1n2
Layseca y Alvarado, Juan de, 121–2
Lazar, Gabriel Lance, 23
Lemos (7th count), 137–8n1
León, Fray Luis de, 5
Lerma (duke), 65–6, 107
Lerner, Gerda, 127n5
libro de buen amor, El, 45, 140–1n2
Lobaco, Josefa, 10
Lope de Vega, Félix Arturo: and *El alcalde Mayor*, 77; and *Las almenas de toro*, 78–9; and *El anzuelo de Fenisa*, 62; and *Arte Nuevo de hacer comedias*, 63; and *Cabalero de Olmedo*, 85; and *El castigo sin venganza*, 20; and courting actresses, 129n20; and *La dama boba*, 45; and Jusepa Vaca, 78–9; and María de Heredia, 128n14; and *Las Mocedades de Roldan*, 79; and *El perro del hortelano*, 46; and punishment, 20; and the *serrana*, 140–1n2; and *La viuda valenciana*, 46; and Zayas, 137–8n1
López, Francisca, 53

Lorde, Audre, 140n14
Lundelius, Ruth, 141n8

Madrid, 23–4, 51, 98, 132nn12, 13
Magdalena de San Jerónimo, María: about, 30; and experience, 31; and false beggars, 34, 135n29; and *la galera*, 30–1, 33–4, 36–7, 107–12, 132–3n16, 134–5n26; and Mary Magdalene, 40; and performance, 38; and prostitutes, 34–5; and unruly women, 39
Magdalene house (Nashville, Tennessee), 105
Magdalene, Mary, 11, 20, 25, 39, 40, 121, 127n3
Magdalen houses: and Casa Pía de Arrepentidas de Santa Magdalena, 30; and containment, 67; and daily routine, 28, 38; defined, 127n3; and exemplarity, 20; and funding, 28; and geographic distribution, 132n15; and Mary Magdalene, 40; and performance, 12, 20, 41; and power, 28; and prostitutes, 20; and punishment, 28, 32–3; and rehabilitation, 12, 127n3. *See also* Casa de Santa María Magdalena de la Penitencia, La; custodial institutions
Malón de Chaide, Pedro, 5
Manzano, Ana, 121
Margaret of the Cross, 139n8
Margarita of Austria (queen), 65, 133–4n21, 139n8
Mariana (of Austria), 11–12
Mariana de San José, 30, 133–4n21
María of Austria (empress), 139n8
Mariscal, George, 4, 131n5
Maroto Camino, Mercedes, 138n4

marriage: and La Casa de Santa María Magdalena de la Penitencia, 26–7; and containment, 52; and *La dama duende*, 46, 52, 59–61, 97; and domestic violence, 64; and education, 86–7; and ideal wife, 68–9, 139n12; and masculine disguise, 77–8; and rehabilitation, 11, 12, 39; and *La serrana de la Vera*, 77, 83–4, 86, 91; and *La traición en la amistad*, 64, 70–1, 73–6, 97; and unruly women, 45; and widows, 13, 47, 48, 60

Martínez, Ana. *See* Baltasara de los Reyes, Francisca

Martínez Galindo, Gema, 134n22

Mary Magdalene, 11, 20, 25, 39, 40, 121, 127n3

masculine roles: and actresses, 96; and masculine woman character, 3, 81–5, 91, 140–1n2

McKendrick, Melveena, 82

Medina de las Torres (duke), 11

Menéndez Pidal, María Goyri de, 140n1

Menéndez Pidal, Ramón, 140n1

Moraga, Cherríe, 140n14

moral behaviour: concern with, 4; and the difference between "good" and "bad" women, 34; and *la galera*, 32; and gender roles, 4–5; and Inquisition, 22; and moral character, 27; and performance, 129n18; and punishment, 41; and *recogimiento*, 21, 24; regulation of, 5; and *La serrana de la Vera*, 14; and social problems, 128n9; and theatre, 11, 99; and urban anonymity, 51; and widows, 46, 50, 61; and women, 61, 65. *See also* social norms; unruly women

Morales, Mariana Vaca de, 78

Morales Medrano, Juan de, 78

moralists: defined, 127n6; and moral behaviour, 5; and rehearsal process, 8–9; and theatre, 5

Moreiras, Alberto, 131n5

motherhood, 82–4, 90, 102, 103, 143n6

mountain woman. *See serrana*

Mozas de la Galera, Las, 100

Mujica, Bárbara, 46

Muñoz, Ana, 82, 83

murderess: and modern criminals, 103, 143n6; and *La serrana de la Vera*, 14, 77, 89–91, 94–5, 142n13; and violence, 13. *See also* roles; violence

Novelas amorosas y ejemplares (Zayas), 137–8n1, 138nn4, 5, 8

Núñez de Guzmán, Pedro, 11

O'Connor, Thomas, 8, 11

Olivares (count-duke), 31, 79

paintings: *Alegoría de la Vanidad*, 11, 129nn22, 23; *Auto de fe en la Plaza Mayor de Madrid*, 130n1; *La Magdalena penitente*, 40–1; onstage, 54; and the Recogidas of Madrid (Mary Magdalene, St Joseph, S. Onofre, St Francis, St John the Baptist, St Gerónimo), 121

Palacios, Francisco, 121

Palomino, Antonio, 121

Parr, James A., 141n7

Paun de García, Susan, 138n4

Peale, C. George, 77

Pellice, Casiano, 3

penitence. *See* rehabilitation

penitentiaries: and the *galera* model, 30; and same-sex relations, 133n19; and the study of women's prisons, 12. See also *galera, la*
Pere, Wan de, 121, 125
Pérez Baltasar, María Dolores, 25, 133n18
Pérez, Cosme, 3, 127n1
Pérez de Colosía Rodríguez, María Isabel, 22
Pérez de Herrera, Cristóbal, 132–3n16, 134n22
Pérez de Montalbán, Juan, 137–8n1
performance: and *auto de fe*, 6–7, 20–1, 128n11, 130n1; and La Casa de Santa María Magdalena de la Penitencia, 19–21, 28–9; and conversion, 20; and custodial institutions, 15, 98; and *La dama duende*, 55–7, 137n11; and exemplarity, 21; and *la galera*, 36–8; and Inquisition, 3, 41; and Madrid, 23–4; and Magdalen houses, 12, 20, 41; and moral behaviour, 129n18; and penitence, 3, 6–7, 128n11; and public hanging, 38; and punishment, 3–4, 6; and the Recogidas of Madrid, 120; and *recogimiento*, 12; and rehabilitation, 3–4, 19–21, 29, 41; and *La serrana de la Vera*, 77, 81–2, 89; and social norms, 131n5; and theatre, 41; and *La traición en la amistad*, 70. See also exemplarity; theatre
performers: and abandoned or orphaned children, 132n10; and punishment, 127n1, 128n14; and rehearsal process, 8–9; and widows, 49. See also actresses
Perry, Mary Elizabeth, 20, 24, 81

Philip IV. See Felipe IV (king)
Pike, Ruth, 33, 131n7, 134n22
Poska, Allyson M., 48, 131n6
poverty: and moral behaviour, 5, 22, 131n7; and *La serrana de la Vera*, 89
power: and *auto de fe*, 6–7; and festivals, 20; and Magdalen houses, 28; and women, 7, 15–16
printing, 37
prisons. See penitentiaries
prostitutes: about, 24; and actresses, 11; and La Casa de Santa María Magdalena de la Penitencia, 25; and courtesans and widows, 49; and custodial institutions, 24; and *la galera*, 34–5, 109–10; and Magdalene house (Nashville, Tennessee), 105; and Magdalen houses, 20; and Mary Magdalene, 40; and punishment, 20; and rehabilitation, 127n3; and roles, 62; and *La traición en la amistad*, 74. See also unruly women
public theatre. See theatre
punishment: and adultery, 47, 131n8; and *auto de fe*, 6–7, 20–1, 128n11, 130n1; and betrayal, 66–7; and branding, 36–7, 135n30; and *El castigo sin venganza*, 20; and *comedia*, 7; and containment, 65–6, 67; and corporal punishment, 13, 20, 28; and cross-dressing, 3; and custodial institutions, 6; and exemplarity, 38, 67; and *la galera*, 12–13, 30, 37–8, 39, 108, 109; and gender, 30–2, 37, 135n27; and human health, 6; and Magdalen

houses, 28, 32–3; and marriage, 64; and modern criminals, 143n6; and moral behaviour, 41; and performance, 3–4, 6; and performers, 127n1, 128n14; and prostitutes, 20; and public hanging, 38; and religious minorities, 22–3; and same-sex relations, 133n19; and *La serrana de la Vera*, 14, 78, 81, 91–4, 97; and sexuality, 22; and sin, 108; and *La traición en la amistad*, 66–8, 71–4; and unruly women, 108–9; and women, 23, 131n8. *See also* rehabilitation

Quevedo, Francisco de, 79, 96, 137–8n1
Quintana, Jerónimo de la, 27, 133n18

Rambuss, Richard, 94, 142n15
Rana, Juan. *See* Pérez, Cosmé
reality television, 103
Recio, Manuel, 25–7, 119–22, 133n17, 134n25
Recogidas of Madrid, the, 119–22
recogimiento: and La Casa de Santa María Magdalena de la Penitencia, 21, 26–9, 40, 98–9; and custodial institutions, 22, 98; and *La dama duende*, 46–8, 50, 59; defined, 21–2; and exemplarity, 21–2; and *galera*, 98–9; and historical texts, 130n2, 130–1n3; and Mary Magdalene, 40; and moral behaviour, 24; and performance, 12; and the Recogidas of Madrid, 121; and rehabilitation, 12; and widows, 46. *See also* containment
rehabilitation: and *auto de fe*, 6–7, 128n11; and branding, 37; and

La Casa de Santa María Magdalena de la Penitencia, 19–21; and *comedia*, 7, 41, 98; and the contrast between real and fictional practices, 98–9; and control, 28; and conversion, 10–11, 20, 40; and custodial institutions, 4; and *La dama duende*, 13, 45, 48, 53, 58–61, 97; and the economic crisis, 23; and the forms of rehabilitation, 19; and *la galera*, 30–1, 33, 34, 38–9; and gender, 40; and gender relations, 39; and Inquisition, 22; and Magdalene house (Nashville, Tennessee), 105; and Magdalen houses, 12, 127n3; and marriage, 11, 12, 39, 45; and performance, 3–4, 6–7, 19–21, 29, 41, 128n11; and plays outside the *comedia*, 100; and prostitutes, 20, 127n3; and Recio's manual, 25–9, 133n17, 134n25; and the Recogidas of Madrid, 119–22; and *recogimiento*, 12; and redemption, 37; and religious life, 12; and *La serrana de la Vera*, 14, 97; and theatre, 15; and *La traición en la amistad*, 14, 97; and transformation, 41; and women, 6, 7. *See also* punishment
Reina, Eufrasia María de, 10
Relación de las cosas de la cárcel de Sevilla y su trato (Chaves), 133n19
religious life: and *beaterios*, 22; and La Casa de Santa María Magdalena de la Penitencia, 26–7; and confession, 40; and conversion, 10–11, 20, 29, 40, 93–4; and correspondence, 31, 134n23; and Magdalene house (Nashville, Tennessee), 105; and Magdalen houses, 12; and nuns, 27, 133n18;

and the Recogidas of Madrid, 119–22; and rehabilitation, 38; and religious heroines, 93–4, 142n14; and Royal Monastery of the Incarnation, 133–4n21; and *La traición en la amistad*, 69

religious minorities: and Inquisition, 22; and moral behaviour, 5; and punishment, 22–3

Rennert, Hugo, 78–9

Reyes Peña, Mercedes de los, 78

Ringrose, David, 23

Riquelme, María de, 10

Rizzi, Francisco, 130n1

Rodríguez, Ana, 27, 119

roles: and masculine roles, 96; and the masculine woman, 3, 81–5, 91, 140–1n2; and prostitutes, 62; and religious heroines, 93–4, 142n14; and social norms, 97; and unruly women, 13, 15; and the vixen, 13, 14, 62–4, 68, 75, 103. *See also* murderess; widow (role)

Romero, Mariana, 10

Royal House of St Mary Magdalene of the Penitence, the, 119–22

Royal Monastery of the Incarnation, 133–4n21

royal women, 102. *See also* Isabel (queen)

Ruano de la Haza, J.M., 136n10

Ruiz de Mendi, Juan, 45, 78

Ruiz, Teófilo F., 20

saints, 30, 94, 121, 125, 142n15

same-sex relations, 133n19

Sánchez Arjona, José, 79, 141n6

Sánchez, Magdalena S., 65–6, 139n8

Scott, Joan Wallach, 127n5

Sellers, Alicia Álvarez, 129n23

serrana (mythological figure), 140–1n2

serrana de la Vera, La (Vélez de Guevara): and actresses, 78–80; and betrayal, 77, 80–1, 88–92, 94, 142nn11, 12; and class, 84–7, 91, 142n11; and clothing, 87; and comedy, 80; composition of, 140n1; and containment, 84, 87; and conversion, 93–4; and exemplarity, 14, 80–1, 84, 87–8, 93–5, 97; genre influences on, 77–8, 79–80, 141n3; and King Fernando, 89–90; and marriage, 77, 83–4, 86, 91; and masculine disguise, 77; and the masculine woman character, 81–5, 91, 140–1n2; and motherhood, 83–4, 90; and the murderess, 14, 77, 89–91, 94–5, 142n13; and performance, 77, 81–2, 89; and punishment, 78, 81, 91–4, 97; and Queen Isabel, 86, 88, 90; and rehabilitation, 97; and religious heroines, 93–4, 142n14; and sexuality, 84–6, 89, 91, 142n11; and social norms, 97; and theatre, 85; and unruly women, 77–8, 141n8; and violence, 77, 78, 94. *See also* Vélez de Guevara, Luis

serrana de la Vera, La (Vélez de Guevara) (by character): Andrés, 89; Fernando (king), 14, 86, 89–90, 92, 94; Gila, 14, 77–97, 141nn2, 8, 142nn13, 14; Giraldo, 81, 82–3, 86, 92; Isabel (queen), 14, 85–6, 88, 90, 92; Lucas, 80, 84–8, 90–1, 142n11

Sessa (duke), 129n20

sexuality: and actresses, 82; and adultery, 131n8, 139n12; and colonialism, 99–100; and

conversion, 29; and courtly love,
140–1n2; and *La dama duende*,
53, 55–6, 57–8; and degrees of
womanliness, 68; and extramarital affairs, 10; and gender,
63; and Jusepa Vaca, 79, 141n5;
and Mary Magdalene, 40; and
penitentiaries, 133n19; problem
of, 132–3n16; and punishment,
22; and *recogimiento*, 21–2; and
Saint Sebastian, 94, 142n15; and
same-sex relations, 28, 133n19; and
seduction, 9–10; and *La serrana de
la Vera*, 84, 84–6, 89, 91, 142n11;
and *La traición en la amistad*, 14,
62–4, 67, 71–2, 74, 139n10; and
veils, 50; and widows, 45, 48–9;
and women's community, 14
Shakespeare, William, 45
Shergold, N.D., 128n14
Siena, Kevin P., 131n6
Sjoberg, Laura, 104
slavery, 37, 66
Smith, Susan, 103, 143n6
social norms: and actresses, 66; and
comedia, 97–8; and the creation of
la galera, 31–2; and *La dama duende*,
97; and domestic problems, 64;
and the economic crisis, 23; and
gender, 97; and the ideal wife,
68–9, 139n12; and identity, 131n5;
and Jusepa Vaca, 94–5, 96–7; and
motherhood, 82–4, 90, 102, 103,
143n6; and public pressure, 99;
and roles, 97; and *La serrana de la
Vera*, 80, 82–4; and theatre, 41; and
La traición en la amistad, 63, 64, 97;
and unruly women, 60–1, 94–5,
104; and women, 7, 12, 15; and
women's communities, 63, 65–6,

67–8. *See also* moral behaviour;
unruly women
social welfare institutions. *See*
custodial institutions
soirees, 138n4
Stradling, R.A., 132n11
Stroud, Matthew D., 63, 69, 140–1n2
Suárez de Figueroa, Cristóbal, 78
sumptuary laws, 9–10
Szabo, Franz A.J., 132n13

Tassis y Peralta, Juan de, 96
Thacker, Jonathan, 135n2
theatre: and agency, 53–8; closing
of, 11–12; and *corrales*, 6, 28, 51;
criticism of, 7–8; and custodial
institutions, 4–6, 11, 28, 99; and
La dama duende, 13, 46, 50–2, 53–6,
60–1; and education, 8; and exemplarity, 8, 20; and iconography,
129n23; and moral behaviour, 11;
and performance, 41; professionalization of, 6, 41; and *La serrana de
la Vera*, 85; and soirees, 138n4; and
unruly women, 14–15, 101. See
also *comedia*; performance
Tirso de Molina, 56, 63, 77, 88,
140–1n2
Tormo, Elías, 129n22
traición en la amistad, La (Zayas):
and containment, 76, 97; and
exemplarity, 63, 97; and gender,
138–9n6; and ideal wife, 68–9,
139n12; and marriage, 64, 70–1,
73–6, 97; and performance, 70;
and punishment, 66–8, 71–4; and
rehabilitation, 14, 97; and religious
life, 69; and role of *engaño*, 71; and
sexuality, 14, 62–4, 67, 71–2, 74,
139n10; and social norms, 97;

staging of, 63, 138n2; study
of, 138n4, 138–9n6; "traición"
defined, 66; translations of,
139n11; and unruly women, 63–4,
68, 71–6; and the vixen, 62–4, 68,
75; and women's communities,
14, 62–77, 139n10. *See also* Zayas y
Sotomayor, María de
traición en la amistad, La (Zayas)
(by character): Belisa, 70–3; Don
Juan, 71–2, 139n10; Fenisa, 14,
62–4, 67–8, 71–6, 97, 139nn6, 10;
Gerardo, 73–4, 139n10; Laura, 65,
68–71, 73–4, 139n10; Liseo, 62,
68–71, 73–4, 139n10; Marcia, 62,
65, 68–74, 139n10
tricksters, 62, 71, 135n29

unruly women: in contemporary
period, 101–4; and criminal actions, 103; and custodial institutions, 98; and *La dama duende*, 13,
58–61; and exemplarity, 98; and
false beggars, 34, 135n29; and
good women, 34; and Jusepa Vaca,
94–5, 96–7; and marriage, 45; and
mass media, 104; problem of, 39,
132–3n16; and roles, 13, 15; and *La
serrana de la Vera*, 77–8, 141n8; and
social norms, 60–1, 94–5, 104; and
theatre, 14–15, 101; and *La traición
en la amistad*, 14, 63–4, 68, 71–6.
See also moral behaviour; prostitutes; social norms
urban design, 23–4, 51, 98

Vaca, Jusepa, 14, 78–81, 94–5, 96–7,
141n4
Vaca, Mariana, 78
Valdés, Fernando de, 6–7, 20

Valdivielso, 140–1n2
Valle (marchioness), 65–6
Valle y Cerda, Teresa de la, 134n24
Varey, J.E., 28, 128n14
Velasco, Sherry, 127n1, 133n19
Vélez de Guevara, Luis: and *La
Baltasara*, 11, 100; and *El diablo
cojuelo*, 140n1; and Jusepa Vaça,
78–80, 96–7; and tragedy, 77, 141n7;
works of, 140n1; and writing style,
141n8. See also *serrana de la Vera, La*
(Vélez de Guevara)
Villacampa, Pasqual de, 122
Villamediana (count), 96
Villanueva (marqués), 79
violence: and domestic violence,
64; and *esturpo*, 142n12; and
gender, 90, 92, 143n6; and modern
criminals, 103, 143n5; and the
murderess, 13; and *La serrana de la
Vera*, 77, 78, 94. *See also* murderess
Vives, Juan Luis, 5, 46, 50, 64–5
vixens: and sexuality, 13; and *La
traición en la amistad*, 62–4, 68, 75;
and women's community, 14
Vollendorf, Lisa, 6, 22, 62–3,
128n10

Weissberger, Barbara F., 141–2n10
Whitby, William M., 141n7
widow (role): and the popularity of
the role, 61. See also *dama duende,
La* (Calderón); roles
widows: and actresses, 49, 53; and
economic issues, 47, 48; and
the etymology of "widow," 50;
and increasing numbers of, 46,
51; and marriage, 13, 47, 48, 60;
and moral behaviour, 46, 50, 61;
and mourning period, 47–8, 51;

and sexuality, 45, 48–9; in Spanish texts, 45–6; and the status of, 48; and virtuous widows, 27, 136n6
Wiesner-Hanks, Merry E., 48
Wilkins, Constance, 63
women: and the degrees of womanliness, 68; and the devil, 137n11; and education, 6; and employment, 110; and exemplarity, 12, 34, 35; and frivolity, 57; and moral character, 27; and power, 7, 15–16; and punishment, 23, 131n8; and rehabilitation, 6, 7; and societal roles, 7, 12, 15. See also gender
women's communities: and actresses, 66; and The Bachelor, 103; and betrayal, 14, 62, 66–7, 73; and confidences, 64; and creation of la galera, 31; and La dama duende, 53–7; and differences between women, 75,

140n14; and economic support, 131n6; existence of, 65–6, 139n8; and Magdalena de Guzmán, 65–6; policing of social norms by, 62–77; study of, 139n7; and La traición en la amistad, 14, 62–70, 72–7, 139n10; and the vixen, 68
workhouses, 33, 135n28
Wunder, Amanda, 50

Yagüe Olmos, Concepción, 12

Zamudio, Beatriz, 30
Zayas y Sotomayor, Fernando, 137–8n1
Zayas y Sotomayor, María de: about, 62, 137–8n1; novelas of, 137–8n1, 138nn4, 5. See also traición en la amistad, La (Zayas)
Zerezo, Mateo, 121
Zorilla, Rojas, 11

Toronto Iberic

1 Anthony J. Cascardi, *Cervantes, Literature, and the Discourse of Politics*
2 Jessica A. Boon, *The Mystical Science of the Soul: Medieval Cognition in Bernardino de Laredo's Recollection Method*
3 Susan Byrne, *Law and History in Cervantes' Don Quixote*
4 Mary E. Barnard and Frederick A. de Armas (eds), *Objects of Culture in the Literature of Imperial Spain*
5 Nil Santiáñez, *Topographies of Fascism: Habitus, Space, and Writing in Twentieth-Century Spain*
6 Nelson Orringer, *Lorca in Tune with Falla: Literary and Musical Interludes*
7 Ana M. Gómez-Bravo, *Textual Agency: Writing Culture and Social Networks in Fifteenth-Century Spain*
8 Javier Irigoyen-García, *The Spanish Arcadia: Sheep Herding, Pastoral Discourse, and Ethnicity in Early Modern Spain*
9 Stephanie Sieburth, *Survival Songs: Conchita Piquer's Coplas and Franco's Regime of Terror*
10 Christine Arkinstall, *Spanish Female Writers and the Freethinking Press, 1879–1926*
11 Margaret E. Boyle, *Unruly Women: Performance, Penitence, and Punishment in Early Modern Spain*